DELA FO

AWARD-WINNING, BEST-SELLING AUTHOR

InJoyness

HOW I STARTED LIVING THE LIFE I WAS MEANT TO LIVE

DELA FOTOOHI

DELA FOTOOHI

AWARD-WINNING, BEST-SELLING AUTHOR

InJoyness

HOW I STARTED LIVING THE LIFE I WAS MEANT TO LIVE

DEDICATION

To my Father, Manuchehr Fotoohi,
I dedicate this book to your memory. I love you, and
forever will keep you in my heart.
I know you are proud of me Pedar.

DELA FOTOOHI

Acknowledgements

My deepest gratitude

To My Family:

My Mom, Farideh, for always encouraging me to pursue my dreams, my husband, Sean, for his unwavering support, my son Dylan for his kindness and humour when I needed it most, my brother, Reza, for being a source of inspiration, Vida, for being my sister from another mister, for being my confidant.

To my extended family and special friends for their love and support.
My heart is full.

To my coaches (in chronological order of their appearance in my journey) for their guidance and direction:
Carlayne Gilbertson
Dr. Azita Sayan
Guillome McMartin
Dr. Behrang Ajam

Dela Fotoohi

James MacNeil

Ahmad Shah Duranai

Meir Ezra

Robert J. Moore

Lori McNeil

Thank you for having faith in me when I did not.

To every single soul that has crossed paths with me, I want to thank you for the lessons you have taught me, for I know that I would not be who I am today, without you touching my life.

In Gratitude & Love

-Dela

TABLE OF CONTENTS

Table of Contents

Foreword

I have done what historically, very few people have been able to do; come back from a long history of drug and alcohol addiction and a life with no purpose, no education, and no hope. I honestly thought my journey was over, and my path was at a dead end until a miracle happened. Therefore, I genuinely understand Dela's story; although she wasn't the one who used alcohol, but she was affected by it.

Dela talks about reaching out to get yourself help, and it brought back some memories from when I was so entrenched in my addiction that asking for help seemed to be the last thing I could do, as the addiction held me hostage.

I do want to mention that being addicted to anything is no way to live, as I have seen some pretty dark days and time – and a lot of time, I just totally blanked out.

I love the fact that Dela's mother decided to bring her and her brother to Canada; although it was a rough ride to achieve, but she stuck with it and made it happen. This is a lot like what I do now, I might have a hard time with something, but I will not give up and keep remembering why I do the things I do.

This reminds me that Dela talks about denial, and I can honestly say I was in denial for many years, thinking no one would know my problems, but to my surprise, I was the last to know that everyone already knew!

DELA FOTOOHI

I am grateful to have the honour to be a part of Dela's book, "InJoyness," as I can relate a lot to her story.

I have been coaching Dela for a while and can say I am truly proud of her as she works very hard to achieve her goals, but like others, it does not come easy to her, but she will not give up!

I would encourage you to read over her "triple-A Success Formula" as she puts in some facts to be implemented in all of our lives, e.g. Admit, Ask, Act, she also has a self-assessment tool that is highly beneficial to everyone.

I am proud to today call Dela a colleague and friend.

Love & Respect

Robert J Moore

Internationally Awarded Bestselling Author

Guinness World Record Holder

INTRODUCTION

If you're reading this book, you have decided that what I have to say is worth your time, and I want to thank you for this.

Someone told me we all have two wolves inside of us! Whichever we feed the most is the one that will get stronger and dominate our thoughts and therefore our actions. I would like to think that most of us, most of the time, intend to feed the GOOD WOLF because we are by instinct, loving, nurturing and peaceful beings that falter only at times to feed the BIG BAD WOLF. The latter is the cause of so many troubles in our lives: you know: despair, envy, deceit, hatred, anger, depression, disease. The more we feed the Bad Wolf, the weaker the Good Wolf will become and with time, he'll be too frail to live on. Graphic enough for you?

It all starts with our thoughts. I say just kill the bad wolf right then and there.

No sense in feeding it. I recognize all negative thoughts as soon as they happen, WE ALL DO. Stop them right then and there!!! Then imagine the Big Bad Wolf and his dangerous sharp teeth and slap him a good slap. Take a deep breath and think of the Good Wolf and give him a loving smile. There! Feel Better?

This is my truth, and I don't care who knows it: there is nothing like the excitement of a new task or the adrenaline rush of an exciting challenge. It is indeed in my temperament to be easily moved by new ideas, which in theory is a positive characteristic, if not for the fact that yours truly has a history of starting projects and then sadly abandoning them. Sounds familiar? Please say, yes!!! Tell me I'm not the sole traveller on the road of the non- follow-through-ers (yes, I just made up a word).

Let's see; there was a time I felt the urge to start Karate. The discipline and fundamentals were fascinating. The Katas looked so enchanting, and the dream of mastering the art was consuming my soul (and I looked super cool in my white Gee). I attended all classes, learnt my Katas, practiced, even learned to count to ten in Japanese!!! I was a real Tiger; for two whole months! And then the novelty wore off. One day I just decided Karate was not for me anymore.

Then, there was the time I decided to learn the piano. After all, playing the keys had been my longtime dream. I enrolled in lessons, and I vowed to become the best I could. I played *The Love Story* over and over. I memorized music notes and practised every night. I was truly a devoted student for eight whole weeks!!! And then the excitement faded away, and playing the piano was no longer my priority.

It's just after 10:30 p.m., and I'm sitting on my office floor, trying to sum up my 48 years of life into the pages of what I hope will become a book. The truth is I have wanted to write a book for a long time. I always thought it would be quite amazing to have written a book, and I have started so many.

To be honest, I probably have ten different versions of a book started in different forms, on loose paper, on Word Doc and on the pages of a multitude of journals. They all started off with a different focus and almost always were left to be continued, but I have never gone back to them. Why I ask myself, is it so difficult to finish what I have started?

I think I know now; after all, I am not Oprah, Berne Brown or Rachel Hollis. Who cares about what a woman with no particular expertise has to say? Who would want to read about me or what I think anyway? Tonight for the first time in my life, I decided that I am worth reading about. No one, not even Oprah (and I love her), has my story. No one in this entire universe has lived my life, and absolutely no one can tell it from my perspective. Because let's face it, no one is me! That's right guys; I am unique, and so is every life experience that I have lived and what I have to tell. It's my story and mine alone.

So here we go, my name is Dela. This is my book, and in writing it, I hope to inspire many of you to love more, to smile more and appreciate more. This is InJoyness, and here is the story of how I started living the life I was meant to live.

How I Started Living the Life I was Meant to Live

Meet the little girl in me with huge insecurities.

I have always thought I had fat legs, that's right. This is the first time I have ever said this. My legs are thick from my ankles all the way to my thighs. Even at my skinniest self, my inner thighs rub together. I have trouble wearing certain shoes because the strap is too bloody tight around my ankles. Zipping up boots gives me stress, and skinny jeans look not so skinny on me. When I was a teenager, I hated my legs. You would hardly catch me in shorts or anything that would expose them. I also despised my feet and toes. Yeah, my toes! I thought they were much too stubby. I would try and make them seem longer by painting them, but with my toenails being mere dots, that would be very difficult to accomplish. I dreamt of long and slender legs; I once spent hundreds of dollars I didn't have on some useless fat and cellulite reduction. I dieted like a lunatic and rubbed my legs with anti-cellulite gels.

My knees, oh my god, don't even get me started on them. Boney knees were my dream. I looked at other girls who had skinny legs, and I secretly wished I had their legs. In my world, girls who had skinny legs had it made. How wonderful life would be if you could just throw on a little skirt or a pair of shorts and some sandals and run out the door? As if thick legs were not enough, I was also blessed with a big behind, not just wide but also protruding (JayLo was not popular then yet). People around me noticed my big booty and made no effort in keeping their comments to themselves.

My maternal genes had also blessed me with a small waistline, which made my big behind look even bigger. Buying Jeans or any kind of pants was a disaster. I had to buy a bigger size that would fit my hips, which meant the waist was always, always too big, which I would try to keep tight with a belt. A disaster!

Oh, let's not forget that I also wanted longer and more slender fingers. Yes, fingers because I also didn't like my hands. As long as I'm spilling it here, let me tell you that as a Persian chick I was also gifted with lots of hair on my body and yes, my face too(my mom finally plucked my unibrow and threaded my stache when I was 16 because I needed to look more French than Middle Eastern, which I will tell you about later). What can I say, I was a very insecure young woman. Insecure, with a load of distorted body image. A body image that prevented me from seeing all that was beautiful about me for years.

Today in my late 40s (Hhmmm, the new 30s), I still have thick legs AND wait for it ... varicose veins to top it off. I wear skirts, dresses and shorts and to be honest; I wish I had all those years. Today my beautiful big bottom is an ASSet (LOL). And my waistline gives me the curvy feminine beauty that I am grateful for.

Today, my once round breasts have succumbed to gravity, and my hands are a testimony of years of Floral Design wear and tear. Today my wrinkles and laugh lines remind me of me gracefully ageing. Today I need glasses to read because squinting no longer works. Today gravity has got a hold of my body parts, and I have surrendered, because honestly, today for the very first time, I have come to realize that I no longer want to waste time longing for what I don't have, but instead, I appreciate what I do have, a strong, healthy body with all the parts still fully functioning.

When I think back on those days, I remember them fondly, for the most part, anyway. Maybe I have the ability to block out bad memories. That's why, I think, in all of my 48 years, I don't remember anyone ever hurting me or scorning me to the degree that I could pinpoint any one incident. If I think real hard, I can think of a few things that maybe at the time burned me or hurt my feelings, but not enough to dread them. What I have learned is that my so-called naivete has helped me to look at the cup, half full. This has helped me, for the most part, to see the good in every person I meet. There was a time during my dark days that I have not been so generous with extending this grace, but those were not my proudest days. Today I am happy to announce that I get reproached from my loved ones for how naively I look at the world because my general outlook is that 99% of the world population is genuinely kindhearted and wants what's best for everyone. It is this same outlook; I'm sure that has attracted my attention to what's good in people. For whatever reason (I like to call it manifesting my own reality, someone else might call it luck), I have never ever encountered anyone who's hurt me.

I mentioned my dark days, and I owe you an explanation. If I am going to take you back to my lowest of lowest moments, I also have to tell you that I was 100% responsible for those days. I have made a lot, TONS of mistakes in the past. For a while, I felt guilt and loads of shame for the mistakes of my past. I did things that I am not proud of. I said words and did things that hurt people. I lied, cheated and betrayed.

A couple of years ago, I participated in a series of self-discovery workshops by Dr. Azita Sayan, which helped me shed major light on my life. What opened up to me was painful but eye-opening. I found out that the number one person I had harmed and betrayed, lied to, cheated, had been me.

A big part of healing from the past was forgiving myself,

#1 for What I had done to me,

#2 for What I had done to others,

#3 for What others had done to me

and

#4 for What I had allowed others to do to me.

Finding my own responsibility in the hurt I had felt was the first step in my healing. I also learned that I would make many more mistakes if I am going to really live. I am willing and ready to make mistakes and learn from them. But the most important thing is to own up to my part, to ask for forgiveness when it is due and to show up with honesty and integrity to do it better using the lessons I learned. Thank you, Dr.Sayan. I cherish you and am forever grateful for all of your teachings.

DELA FOTOOHI

MY YOUTH

Yes, just like everyone else my age that lived in Iran, I have had my share of pain. My childhood was turbulent, with events that were out of my control. Revolutions happen, governments change, poverty, war, addiction, The usual stuff, You know!!!

My dad was a teacher; he was a good man who drank a lot. He was a part-time drunk during the school year and a full-time summertime drunk that woke up to his Vodka by his bedside. By the time I was a teenager, his drinking had driven me away from him, and he no longer impressed me. I was happy to stay away and, as a matter of fact, cherished the times he was away. He was very much isolated from the rest of us, sleeping alone and spending his hours in bed with his bottle and music and cigarettes and his thoughts. It was a very sad part of my life, and I hardly think about it. I saw the battle between my parents and my mom's efforts to make him stop drinking in vain, and it never dawned on me that he had chosen this life and did his best to live it. I loved him, and to this day, thinking about his struggles brings me to tears. I wish I had more time with him to get to know him. He was a great man who had lots of friends that liked him. I feel sad about the hard life he led and how short his life was, but I understand his life on earth ended according to his contract as will mine one day.

No regrets, though! Growing up in an alcoholic home has led me to this moment in life and has allowed me to live life and experience it in a different way. Understanding about the disease of Alcoholism and how it can affect generations has been eye-opening, and I have been able to dig deep and look inward and discover my own self, and I am grateful for that. I see the blessings in the way I grew up and cherish the memories I have with my dad. In many ways, I am very similar to him, a loner at heart, but with plenty of friends, compulsive with addictive behaviour. At times, I drank in secret, and at parties, I drank excessively to the point of vomiting. I smoked pot, at first to join in the party, but slowly I started buying my own and panicked when my stash was going dry. I was a pothead for a few years. I quit every night at the feeling of nausea, and the next day craved a draw and searched the opportunity for the high. I smoked in the privacy of my car, in my bathroom, perched on the edge of the bathtub so that I could reach the vent unit above the stall (always afraid one day I would fall and injure myself). The high gave me a sickening feeling of fear and helplessness. I was in denial of my dependence, because after all, "pot is not addictive" (LOL). I convinced myself that it was okay to smoke pot in moderation as long as it did not interfere with my life. But when I started to forget appointments and missed commitments, I resented my weakness. The thought of living without it was scary; I needed it to get me through the day, to get me creative, allow me to relax, have fun, work, rest ... sleep. Plain and simple, I was scared I wouldn't be able to cope if I quit smoking pot. To be quite honest, I have no idea how I had gotten to that stage. I always prided myself on my strength and resilience and always judged dependence on anything remotely addictive, whether it'd be substance or other people. In retrospect, I now believe that I went through this experience to learn a thing or two about addiction and the compassion and empathy the addict needs to heal. Even during the time, I smoked several times a day, denial, denial, denial. No way I was addicted, not to anything or anyone.

AHA! Wait a minute! This just hit me!!!!

Addiction is a form of control of fear, right? I mean, I smoked pot because I thought I was going to feel better because while sober, I was too afraid to face whatever I was trying to forget. For some odd reason, I thought what I had to face was too scary or too much for me to handle. Looking back (and this would be way before I started drinking or smoking as a coping mechanism), I found myself at a time when being seen and admired was my fix. I craved validation, and I would try and get it, even if it meant giving my time, my love, all of myself. I needed to be noticed to feel worthy. I was afraid of not being seen. Since

I had no self-worth, I feared no one would love me, and so I got my version of love by getting the fix I needed, with no values or boundaries. I let countless people walk all over me and use me as a pretty but valueless doormat just so I could hear them say things like, "You're so beautiful," "You are such a nice person," "I don't know what I would do without you," as they wiped their feet on me. I was addicted to attention, approval, and validation. I did many things I didn't want to do, but because I didn't want to be judged by someone, I did them anyway. To this day, I am still aware and working on this latter issue. I pray that by the time this book ends, so will my addiction to the approval of others.

As it goes, I was meant to become a doctor, at least in my parents' opinion. They all called me Doctor Dela for years. Looking back now, I have no idea why they would think that. I don't think I had any of the typical characteristics of a kid who is destined to become a healthcare professional if that's even a thing. Who knows, maybe contrary to what I think I know of my parents' child-raising intellect, they were hoping to manifest their dream in me. All I know is that up to the age of 18, that dream was still alive and thriving, and I had it in my heart that I was going to become Dr. Dela, even to the degree of dreaming of Doctors Without Borders. During my second year of university, when I knew that it might cost me a whole lot more than just winging it before the exam to pass the courses, I decided to pull a fast one and tried the Army. Yes, that would be my answer to fame, fortune and service to the country. I would apply to the Canadian Armed Forces, study while in service and get my medical degree and eventually say goodbye to the military and start my own practice. Budda boom, budda bing! Right? Wrong!!!

Some things are not meant to happen the way you plan them. Even after I did the Armed forces assessment test, which happened to be a no-brainer or at least that's the way I remember it, my mom decided we were moving to another town, so that she could go back to school and get her Canadian bachelors of education degree. She was 47 then. Even as I am saying it now, I feel that I did not do her justice when I considered her old at that age. So off we went to another town, and I left my army dreams behind and kissed my worldwide humanitarian project goodbye. Interestingly, (wink, wink) it just so happened that I was placed on probation for a year and I decided that instead of telling my mother, I would let her believe that I was sacrificing and taking a year off to support her and my brother, while she went back to school. WOW, how deceitful my young mind was!!! Holy cow! I never told my mom what happened that year, for all I know, she may have been suffering from guilt at the thought of her teenage daughter having to work full-time while she studied. That would have felt utterly awful for a parent. Shoot! Sorry, Mom!

Eventually, a year later, I went back and got a degree in Zoology. Seriously? Zoology? What for you ask? Alright, don't judge me, but that's all I could get into, considering how low my GPA was.

Can anyone explain to me why even after the disastrous second year in science, it didn't occur to me that maybe this wasn't my thing and that maybe it was time to find my strong suit? But the hard-headed individual that I was wanted to prove herself and stick it to the man. Finally, in my fourth year trying to pull the marks, I decided that I would have to swallow my pride and confess to the supreme Mother. I remember the conversation; it was in the car. I don't know if she was actually sitting beside me or not. I don't remember looking at her. Could it be that I was avoiding her eyes? I broke her heart that day when I told her I was not going to be a doctor after all. I think she saw all her dreams crushed at that moment. And for me, that was a moment of exhilarating relief. I was finally free! Now, what???

It seems as if that moment was the start of a never-ending task of trying to prove myself.

THE BRUTAL TRUTH

"Healing always involves facing truths we'd rather not face ... and accepting responsibility, we'd rather not accept."

- Dr. David Hawkins

I had a boss and a kind of mentor that I loved, and I hated. I loved him because he believed in me and trusted me. I hated him because his brutal honesty to call me out made me cry on more than one occasion. He once told me that "my character was flawed." So certain of my command of the English language, I laughed and replied, "Is flawed even a word?" "WHATEVER," I thought!!!

I resented him for saying that, thinking, "How dare he?" "Didn't he know how hard I worked for him?" "Didn't he realize how good he had it with me working my butt off for him?" "Why would he say that about me?" "And after all, how could he know that???"

Hmmm!!! I wonder what gave that away about my character? Was it my constant demand for attention and validation? Was it my general ingratitude, or my obvious resentment for others' success and my lack thereof? Or any of the above?

I was 23 years old and spent most of my time obsessing about the size of my bottom and the shape of my eyebrows. I was struggling in school, with loans stacking up and still very much unsure of what I wanted to do with my life. I had a mediocre sales job, and almost non-existent self-esteem, a load of misery that was weighing me down and bad eating habits. The more wine I drank, the worse it got. My attitude towards life was: everyone needs to be nice to me, and if you were not, may God strike you with lightning and misfortune, and if that didn't happen, you would be in my " worst person ever" list until I found grace to forgive you. My brother was one of those poor souls. What made his predicament even more difficult for him was that he also needed me to advocate for him. So my relationship with him was one of push and pull.

My brother was born when I was six. By the time I was in grade 3, I was entirely in charge of taking care of my brother while my mom was at work. I loved him but resented the fact that I was responsible for him. And sadly, my remedy was to hit him to take out my frustrations. When he was four, he told me that he would revenge himself when he got older. I always believed him and awaited the day.

NEW HORIZONS

"The Best is yet to come."

- William Shakespeare

I should mention that I lived in France from the time I was 14 until just after my 17th birthday. (Mais oui, bien sur que je parle français).

Thinking back now at my exposure to French culture, I look at those years as the most fascinating time of my young life, a time of daze, amazement and confusion that hit me like a tornado. After all, I was a teenage refugee from a third world country. (Here I need to include this disclosure that despite popular opinion of some Iranian compatriots who might argue that Iran "was once on the verge of becoming the modern gem of the Middle East," I am talking of the era of the Ayatollahs when Iran was war-stricken, poor and very much backward in many ways). Nonetheless, at 14, in 1987, I entered France with a few built-in beliefs about boys and girls in general, a handful of love affairs under my belt, a steaming kissing experience (tongue and all), a typical Persian girl unibrow, unwaxed legs and not a word of French.

I arrived in France, in a panic to conquer all my french counterparts, to rise up to the highest mountains and to win them all over. I was going to shine like I had at home, despite all my deficiencies, all my lack, I was going to make my dreams come true. I had practised the scene in my mind. I was sitting at an outdoor cafe, sunglasses and all, basking in the sun, drinking whatever, chatting to whomever, in a made-up language that only kids can muster up. I was merely copying a woman in a picture I had seen; it must have been the picture of a relative abroad that was hacked in my mind and was the epiphany of what freedom would look like. Even at 14, I knew that one day I would live the life of that woman in the photograph.

The days leading up to our departure were filled with secrets. Secrets and melancholy. Secret because no one should know we were leaving the country and the melancholy of not being able to say goodbye. I would leave behind life as I had known. That was 33 years ago. That would be the last time I ever saw Iran.

Our plane landed in Paris on a sunny day in April 1987. I had left behind, my father, my friends, my relatives, my home, my culture, my language and everything that was familiar to me. My mother was just 40 years old and had to have been scared out of her mind, but she never showed it. She was emigrating with two kids, no money, no job, just a dream, a burning desire for her kids to have a better life and a promise of a better future.

My aunt Susan had been living in France for a couple of years, and we would be staying with her until we got on our feet. Everything was beautiful and exciting in Paris. From day one, I was in awe of my new life. The differences were unsettling to my young mind. I adapted fast and furious, learning the language and trying to fit in.

And then one day, there I was, right there in that photograph, sitting at the cozy cafe, alone with my cup of coffee, writing in my journal. And I had won. I had manifested a dream.

My life had changed. I played tennis on the tennis grounds. I boarded with the french at their summer home by the sea. I rode a bike to the beach where I suntanned topless. I picked fresh flowers and wild berries in the garden. I ate french cheese and creme fraiche and basked in gratitude at my good fortune. I learned French at an impressive speed and adapted to my new way of life in a matter of just a few short months. By the time summer was over and September rolled in, I was ready to go back to school and enrolled in grade 8, just one year behind my normal grade. My first day was very blurry, a glimpse of some school staff taking me to my first class and introducing me to the students as a newcomer with very little French.

I can't remember much from those days, except that a couple of friends that took me on as their protege, smoked cigarettes and sang along to Papa Don't Preach from Madonna and impressed me with their ability to sing in English. Slowly I was becoming a part of the tribe. I had very few friends but was well respected, and no one messed with me. I worked hard and was well mannered, and my hard-working attitude impressed the teachers.

I survived and passed into high school.

Le Foyer

Before our visitor's visa ran out, Mom applied for refugee status, and we stayed in France in the hopes of making it home, at least temporarily. Once you were in the system, the government dispersed refugees to different regions. And, as for our little trio, we were shipped to the province of Bretagne in the Northwestern corner of France to a little town called Rennes. We were received by Madame Manghi, a short stubby french woman, who looked and acted like a school principal. She was in charge of the hostel that we were assigned to. Le Foyer looked like at one point; it had been a dormitory. The rooms were modestly furnished like those of a military base, with a bed, table and chairs and a closet. There was also a small sink. Toilets and showers were shared with the other residents.

There were two floors. The ground floor was for single men, and the second floor was for families and single women.

My first few nights were spent alone in a single room. That is the room where I spent countless hours looking up French words in my not so "petit" Petit Robert. It took so long to read and understand any one given paragraph that I studied well into the night most nights. After a short time, our family was given a large room where all three of us could be together, which made me very happy. There was also a large kitchen which allowed families to cook for themselves and eat there if they wanted. There was no shortage of nationalities in Le Foyer. Afghan, Iranian, Cambodian, Vietnamese, Laotians, Algerian, Taiwanese, Bulgarian, Chinese, African, we all lived under the same roof, cooked in the same kitchen, ate at the same table. And all of us basked in the glory that one day we would make it.

Down on the first floor, there was a recreation room equipped with I imagine a variety of entertainment games. The one I remember with fond memories is the ping pong table. It was hardly ever free, as players would spend hours testing their ambition and their talent against the very best of the pack, who usually went back and forth between the Cambodians and Laotians, and then there was Monsieur Lou, the Moroccan wise man of the Tribe. Mr. Lou knew everything about everyone. He spent all of his time in the games room, smoked cigarettes and played ping pong like a pro. I learned to play ping pong from the oriental teenage boys who would take the time to let me practise, cheered me when I smacked the ball and laughed when I missed. I had fun with that crowd; it was an easy crowd, no pretense, no superiority, no fuss. We all spoke very little french, had not much in common, and yet we were all connected in deeper ways than imagined. We connected in our melancholy, in our loneliness, in our newness. We connected in the only way we knew how: that none of us belonged there, and we all so desperately wanted to belong.

Le Foyer also had a language tutor: Francois, a tall, handsome man in his twenties, who offered extra help to anyone who went to him. I liked him and spent as much time as possible in his office.

The time we spent in that hostel, although short, offered me a new view of people from other countries. I look back now and realize that I learned so much in regard to other nationalities and how this would play a role in my integration into Canada, just a few short years later.

Our very first Christmas holiday at Le Foyer was wonderful. There were decorations, music, dancing. We dressed up and danced all night.

What freedom to dance without a care! I truly felt free that night. I felt true joy.

I met my first official boyfriend here, a boy from Laos, dark, handsome and a very sweet boy whom I got caught kissing and had to say goodbye to. Not because I was banned seeing him, but because I used that as an excuse to stop seeing him. He was heartbroken. He gave me a gift, a pair of navy blue trousers. Hmmm, I have no idea why! It seemed odd and very out of the ordinary to get pants from your 16-year-old boyfriend.

My next "boy venture," was a man from Chile. He was a singer in a band. I can't remember where I met him. But I remember he invited me to a wedding he was playing at. I felt sort of special to be the date of the handsome singer. After the wedding, as we rode in his car into the deep of the forest, I thought I was in trouble. We stopped, and I knew I needed him to know this was not okay. When he leaned over to fondle my breasts, I knew I needed to speak up NOW or forever hold my peace. I asked him to take me home right away, and he did. Do you know something? I know for a fact that God has been watching over me all my life because I have put myself in a pickle on more than one occasion.

We met other Iranians and began slowly feeling less and less like foreigners as we found our way around town and became more familiar with the french ways. My first opportunity to work was as a Cigarette Girl at the circus that had come to town. I wore a tie and was extremely proud of myself for working. I was 15.

There was a french family that kind of adopted us too, the Ledoux family.

Marie France Ledoux was a beautiful blonde woman with a heart of gold. Her husband wasn't really a talker, but kind also. I really don't know how they came into our lives or if we came into their lives. Either way, knowing the Ledoux family gave me a sense of belonging that gave me hope that maybe I could actually make France a home. Our very first Christmas at the Ledoux family was a 4-hour feast at the dinner table that introduced me to the fine French cuisine. I was in awe of the ornaments on the Christmas tree and the festive decorations in every corner of the house; I was delighted by the smell of pine and the sight of presents under the tree. This was my very first glimpse of what Noel looked like.

In a short time, we were able to rent a small apartment and move into our very first home. It was on the second floor of a short building and had all the amenities we needed.

And that's where we met the missionaries for the first time.

The two men in white shirts, dark suits, tall, handsome and clearly American, and they wore name tags. In retrospect, they were really young, early twenties, I think, but to me, they looked much older.

They came to our door, we opened the door and invited them into our home and then slowly into our hearts. The missionaries were young men from The Church of Jesus Christ of Latter-Day Saints, aka The Mormon Church. They were in France on a two-year mission to introduce their faith.

One day I came home, and our apartment was filled with young men in suits sitting on our couch, and next, they were eating Persian food at our table. They called my mother, Mom, and we adopted them as part of our family. Some left and new ones came. My favourite was Ralf, a young funny Robert Redford type. He taught us to bake chocolate chip cookies and pancakes. He was like my big brother. Ralf left soon after his mission was over, and that was the last time we ever saw him.

Whenever one of the missionaries was leaving, he made sure to introduce his successor. I always worried about who would replace our missionary. They ate at our table, met our friends, together we laughed, we cried and prayed.

One of these missionaries was Jessie, a tall Canadian that came into my life and stole my 16-year-old heart and made it his. He was tall and slim and wore glasses. He was kind and attentive. The missionaries were not allowed to have romantic relationships while on the mission. So we had our moments of undeniable attraction and suffered in secret. I can't remember how he confessed to me about his affection, but I think Jessie was a key element in my mom's decision to start another journey, this time to Canada. As we packed all our belongings into three suitcases, I can only imagine what thoughts went through my then 42-year-old Mother's mind. I don't know too many women who have had the courage she had to once again migrate with two children, this time across the globe to yet another country, with no one to protect her, no money and no prospects. My friend and her family had emigrated to Canada a couple of years back, and they had taken the route we were going to take, using the same smuggler who would get us flown into Canada with fake passports, but after that, there were no guarantees. My friend and her family lived in Toronto and would let us stay with them when we got there. The journey to Madrid, Spain, was going to be on a train. We said goodbye to the few friends we had that we could trust. And the missionaries and Jessie. They had come to the train station to see us off.

DELA FOTOOHI

THE PASSAGE

"What would life be if we had no courage to attempt anything?

-Vincent Van Gogh

The train ride into Madrid was a long overnight one.

We found a private cab and settled in for the long haul. We would travel with our travel documents into Spain.

Halfway through the night, two men joined our small cab, and Mom was up the entire night in case they tried any funny business. It was almost dawn when they left, and Mom finally relaxed.

I loved Madrid; I had been there just about a year before with my school. It was a new experience for me to be there this time with my family passing through.

The man who was smuggling us met us at the train station. He was driving a BMW and talked about going to the Canary Islands. I remember thinking, "I wonder if we can trust him?" I had never heard of the Canary Islands. To this day, the Canary Islands always remind me of an uncertain time of my life. I may go there one day, but then again, maybe I don't want to. He drove us to a room with two beds on the second floor of a boarding apartment building right in downtown Madrid. He took the passport-size photos that Mom had brought and said he would come back the next day. We had planned to stay in Madrid for a couple of days and then fly out to Toronto with our fake French passports. With no plans at all, we decided to go sightseeing.

There was a MacDonald's nearby, where we ate and walked around the neighbourhood. Money was short, and we needed to be prudent.

I remember when the man came back and fixed the French passports right in front of our bewildered eyes. He lifted the laminate and replaced the existing photo of some poor woman who was probably devastated that her passport had been lost, and then placed mom's photo in its place and glued the laminate back. It was flawless. Mom became Marie Lefevre, travelling with her five-year-old son, my ten-year-old brother and her niece, me. I had my own passport with my fake photo representing a twenty-something-year-old french girl. I had to play the part. So the man suggested that I should try and look older. So we spent a day, plucking my brows, dying my hair auburn to make me pass as French. For the first time ever, we were threading my ever so hairy face along with my Persian girl stash. I remember feeling very vulnerable at that moment. Threading had been a ceremony in Iran, done to girls, on the eve of their marriage. It was a very sacred virtue that set girls and women apart. I was so happy to get rid of the mustache and the unibrow finally, so happy in fact that I didn't give a damn about traditions at that moment.

Once the passports were ready, it was just a matter of waiting to see when we could fly out. Word was that immigration agents at the Madrid Airport were becoming very vigilant about illegal travellers.

So we were advised to take a different route and fly out of Lisbon, Portugal and fly into Montreal instead of our final destination, Toronto.

If at 17 years old, I had any hesitation, I don't remember. I just know that I trusted Mom so much in her abilities, that fear and doubt did not even cross my mind. As far as I was concerned, we were on an adventure – one that would take me closer to Canada and one day soon to reunite with Jessie. So it was decided that we would travel into Portugal with our new fake passports. It had also been decided, by our smugglers, that my brother was too young to matter to the immigration agents at the airport, so they left the picture of the little boy untouched and assured us that would not be an issue. I can't remember for the life of me why that last step was left undone. But it was so.

So off we went, on a train to Lisbon, Portugal. The taxi driver who would take us to our hotel took the long way to overcharge us, our first introduction to Portuguese hospitality.

My first impression of Lisbon was that it was old and beat up. Our accommodation was in downtown Lisbon. There was a large square not too far from our hotel with hundreds of pigeons. My brother had fun with them. I still have some photographs from that day. Later we would take the train to the beach, and I spent a few hours sunbathing. The memory of that delicious afternoon would stay with me to this day. The sun was warm, and I had the privacy of my own little island as I laid down on a large rock not too far from the shore.

The departure day finally arrived, and we were off to the airport. We were instructed by our guy to speak only french as our passports introduced us all as French nationals. In retrospect, nothing comes close to the fear my mom must have been feeling about the journey we were about to take. After all, she was pretending to be someone she wasn't to gain illegal access into Canada. With no one to accompany us, no money, no support and no English, okay maybe some, mostly academic, not enough to converse, it must have been daunting. I won't let her read this part, lest she gets offended by my claim.

As we waited in line to go through the checkpoint at the Portuguese airport, my heart was racing, not sure of that of mom's. My brother and I spoke fluent french with practically no accent, which made the claim to be french most believable.

Once on the plane, the wait was excruciating. Mom thought that at any moment now, the police would come and arrest us. Time was standing still, and we were not moving.

I remember how nervous Mom was. She was scared, and worried. What if they know and that's why they are holding the plane. Finally, the plane started on the runway, and we could breathe.

I don't remember what I was thinking exactly at that moment, but I know the anxiety of yet another new chapter was too big for my young mind.

I don't remember much of the 7-hour flight.

We were instructed to destroy our fake passports before we got off the plane. So just about an hour before landing, I went into the bathroom and ripped my passport into tiny little pieces and flushed it down the toilet. I felt so vulnerable, that was the feeling, yes that's set. It's funny, I now look back, and I realize that I have been much too familiar with vulnerability! Wow, now, this is an epiphany!!!

I knew in that little bathroom stall that I had absolutely no idea of what was awaiting me once we landed. The sick feeling of uncertainty and insecurity of relying solely on the mercy of a strange country with a strange new language was overwhelming, and I was terrified.

My mom relied on my strength far too much; I felt that as a burden and I tried so hard to be a strong companion I had promised her I would be almost three years ago when she told me for the first time that we were leaving Iran for good. I needed her to know that she could count on me. So I wiped my tears and went back to my seat and reassured her that I had done what I was supposed to do.

The Grand Canadian Entrance

"But if we hope for that which we see not, then do we with patience wait for it."

- Romans 8:25

We were supposed to land in Toronto, but for reasons given to us by the smuggler, Montreal would be our port of arrival into Canada.

Once we landed, we followed the crowd towards the gates. As I write these words, I can feel my heart racing, with the anxiety I felt as we approached the counter. "Passports," the agent announced. "No passport," Mom said in a low tone of voice. The agent looked unamused. "Passports." He said louder, to which Mom replied, "No passport." I wanted to cry. I was ashamed of my vulnerability at that moment, and I didn't want to be there. The agent yelled: "No passport, No Canada."

My mom, the superwoman, the most heroic woman I knew, the superhero who had dragged her two kids across the world this far, was tired. I saw the weight of the world on her shoulder as she dropped her bag onto the floor and said as loud as she could: "We are tired, we have no passports, we are refugees." And she lost it, tears rolled down her face, and I was crying. The agent said to wait. He left us there. Mom looked at me and said, "Don't worry. It's going to be alright." We weren't going anywhere, that she was sure of. There was no way they were going to turn us away. We had no place to go other than in through the gate into Canada. This was just a game.

Within a few short minutes, we were escorted through the gates into a separate hallway and then into a waiting room with lots of chairs. There were a few people sitting there, but for the most part, it was empty.

At first glance, I recognized the two faces of the young men who were sitting there. Not like I knew them, but that I was sure they were Iranian too. It's funny how Iranians can pick each other out from a crowd, something in the eyes. I don't know how, but if you ask any Iranian, they will tell you this.

We waited for what seemed like an eternity.

My task was easy, keep my mouth shut, forget I speak any French. We would also keep the fact that we had lived in France for the past three years, to ourselves.

The rest was Mom's responsibility, which she was handling like a champ. We carried no ID, which meant that the information we gave, had to be accepted by the immigration agents as the truth. They had brought in an interpreter. He helped fill out some forms with basic information.

Side note: my Persian date of birth was incorrectly translated that day into the Latin calendar, and as a result, I have been stuck with the wrong birthday ever since, which means that all my official documents have my date of birth as May 9th, when I was actually born on April 21st. Just trying to explain this to Canadians has been a hurdle in itself, because obviously, your life's celebration is not to be taken lightly in modern society. Amazing how many Iranian-born people around me also deal with dual birth dates as if it's just a normal thing to let this oversight go since it's way too much trouble for just a little thing. After all, it's just a few days different!!!! Ha?!?!

But still, it's more than just going out on my actual birthday to celebrate and having to show ID to get a free dinner, and your ID says it's not actually your birthday!!! Although this would suck big time, so I would never put myself in this situation. It's more than that; it seems it just added just a little more lie to my real identity.

For obvious reasons, though, I have always been bothered by this. Because look, it's been 30 years, and I just had an Aha moment. Why did I not try to correct this mistake? Why did I not think that my identity had enough value all these years to put in the effort to correct this shortcoming? Interesting!!!

So now, I feel like I have had an awakening of some sort. This is a thing that I have to do for ME, for my own respect and satisfaction. It would be nice to fill out a form and actually write down April 21st in the Date of Birth section. Anyways, that's another battle for another time, and I think I have engrossed you in its details long enough. Sorry!

So back to the airport waiting room/hall. I can't remember how long we sat there, but I have it on good authority that it was at least six hours before we were finally allowed to leave the airport. It was nearly 6:00 a.m., and we left the airport to find a bus that would take us to Toronto.

That was August of 1989, and I was just 17 years old.

RESILIENCE AND ADVERSITY

"We don't grow when things are easy; we grow when we face challenges."

- Unknown

It's amazing what we accomplished in such a short time. School was to start in a few weeks. We stayed with some old friends for a few days before Mom decided we'd better find our way, and we found The Serjourne House, a temporary stay for newcomers at a church near The Eaton Centre in the downtown core. I have fond memories from those days as short as it was, it was my introduction to Canadian life, and I met some of the nicest people there. There was a piano in the main hall, and I practised one of the only two tunes I knew. It made me feel superb. Not too far away is where Mom, my brother and I tried banana splits for the first time, and we laughed, and we rejoiced that we had finally made it to this wonderful destination.

Only a few days in, Mom found a part-time job at a small dry cleaner's. The Church was decent but not ideal, and we wanted our own place. Our first Canadian home was a bachelor basement apartment with a low ceiling on the Danforth. It was furnished with second-hand furniture, the walls covered with ugly wallpaper and the small kitchen was old but equipped with the necessities in working condition. We bought a bunk bed for me, and my brother and mom had a bed that was tucked behind our couch that made up the sitting area right in front of the TV.

We ate at the small kitchen table and were entirely proud to have a home after such a short amount of time. In order to get into school, I had to do an assessment test to place me into the proper grade. I can't remember how I found out about the place and how I got there all by myself. All I know is, I now think back at the resolve of my young self and am utterly impressed at my independence and determination.

I was able to return to High School and pick up where I had left off before leaving France. I was now anticipating an entirely different beast called English as a second language, aka ESL.

If you ask me now, I have no idea how I was able to sit in class and listen to Chemistry, Biology, Math all in a language that was so new to me. Not to speak of reading Hamlet and actually understanding it. How did I do this?

Denial

"When you know better, you do better."

- Maya Angelou

My most painful memory is the day I got a detention!!!

It turned out, if you were late to homeroom for the third time, you would get a detention. This, to me, was an insult. "I never get a detention, this sort of thing doesn't happen to me; I'm a good student!" So I burst into tears, and the attending teacher asked me why I was there, to which I replied that I didn't know!

"I didn't know"... the words that have set me back so many times. Throughout my life, I have used these words, as if they somehow excused my failures and shortcomings. I would like to, right at this very moment, confess this with honesty and courage, that there were many times in my life that I made the wrong decision fully knowing what I was doing and how my actions would hurt others and myself, but I did them anyway. I have no excuse other than I should have known better. A few years ago, I learned to take 100% responsibility for my life and therefore stopped all blaming and complaining. I learned to stop pointing my finger at others and to look at the three that were pointing in my direction. I think that was probably the biggest and the most important lesson. I see now that the statement "I didn't know" was valid when I was a child when perhaps I touched a hot pan and burned myself because I truly didn't know.

Later on, I used "I didn't know" to get me out of trouble when I got caught doing something I wasn't supposed to. And eventually, they became my way out of every trouble I got into. Funny. I do think I heard from someone that I should just do it, and if I got caught, I should just say, "I didn't know." The truth is every time I said I didn't know, I should have known better because I could have asked questions and found out the best way, or the best route, or the best method.

Come to think of it, the last time I used "I didn't know" as an excuse, it cost me a very hefty loss. A while ago, I was enrolled in an incredibly pricey self-development program that included six one-on-one consultations. As a part of the agreement, if any one of the items agreed on in the contract was broken, I would lose a consultation. Well, when I found out that I had broken a rule and therefore would lose one of my sessions, guess what my argument was to myself!!! Yes, you guessed it: "I didn't know," I told myself. The truth is, I should have known because I should have read the contract I signed and taken every item seriously. Losing that session for me was one of the biggest lessons of this course. The fact that I didn't know was and had been 100% my own responsibility. From that day on, I paid attention. Today, I read contracts semi-carefully and make notes of important dates. I do my homework, and I get ready. I ask questions and ask for clarification when I don't understand because at the end of the day, what I don't know can cost me dearly, and I don't mean just money. I heard Oprah quote her teacher Maya Angelou that *"When you know better, you do better."* I no longer beat up on myself for past mistakes because I now know better than I did then. I just know now not to use "I didn't know" as an excuse. I am always learning. You do better when you know better.

DELA FOTOOHI

VALIDATION

"My goal is not to be better than anyone else but to be better than I used to be."

- Dr. Wayne Dyer

My high school years were far from normal, now that I think about them — 1986 to 1991, 5 years over three continents and three countries, in three different languages. I was always trying to fit in it seems, spending more time with my trusted dictionary than worrying about being popular, trying mostly to prove myself and competing with my fellow classmates regardless of whether or not the study matter was in my mother tongue, finding out in desperation that I had to work harder and longer if I was going to make it. And if not, then I had to be nicer and more accommodating to get the approval anyway I could. I did make a couple of friends, although no long-lasting relationships.

I have to confess here that apart from a handful of my childhood friends I grew up with, I have very little memory of any other friends I made along the way. I wonder now if subconsciously I chose to give them little storage space in my brain because they were not important to me or that I was afraid of losing them, so I chose to forget. In other words, I went with "out of sight, out of mind, so what is the point?".

At any rate, some of my highschool affiliations are on my FB, and apart from the occasional likes and feed, they have no impact on my life and vice-versa. I must mention that there are a few people, and they know who they are that I hold very dear to my heart, and I know will always be a part of my life and have impacted me in so many ways and will never ever be forgotten under any circumstances.

As a part of moulding into my new life, as soon as I could, I got a job. With very minimal spoken English, my first job was as a busboy at a Greek restaurant on the Danforth, not too far from where we lived.

I hated the job from day one, but I showed up, and cleaned tables, poured water, carried dishes and did whatever else they told me to do. One night, an Iranian family was sitting at a table, and they offered me a job at their shoe store. I took it immediately without hesitation. At $4 an hour, I was laughing.

I worked a few hours a week and went to school.

I met a set of twins, Mel and Robyn, who welcomed me with big hearts and even bigger smiles. They called me Del and adopted me as their sister. And there was Matthew, my die-hard fan for a short while. I may have broken his heart when I told him I only wanted to be friends. And despite all my vulnerabilities, to be quite honest, I have never experienced any meanness or bullying. I think I just never gave it a second thought as if I was not open to that sort of a thing.

Soon after we moved to Toronto, my Mormon boyfriend, who was back home in Canada from his two-year mission, flew in to visit me. With no more mission enforced boundaries between us, this was a new dynamic, and I was clueless. Jessie spent a few days in Toronto and was heading down to Utah to pursue his education at university. As we talked, our young minds planned and decided for me to join him there, and I would study something. I don't remember now what it was.

Mom was absolutely opposed; she was not about to let her daughter get out of her sight. We decided I would go after I graduated from high school. And Jessie left, and that was the last time I ever saw him. As it turned out, I was not ready to follow him.

I broke my commitment to him a few short months after he left Toronto. I was still so immature and so eager to date others, and I met the next best thing, and his name was Matt. Matt was in his mid-twenties, Iranian background, Mormon and very nice to my family and me.

We met at church one Sunday, and so I thought in my young 18-yr-old-mind that I was going to marry him. I look back now and can't help but wonder why it was so easy for me to get so attached so fast. I think I can psychoanalyze myself and conclude that I suffered from fear of abandonment or something along those lines. But then, also as quickly as I fell in love, I was out of love and on to a new love. It was as if I was scared of wasting time and was playing catch up. Matt was much older, more experienced, and had a business. Pretty quickly, I was working at his pizzeria, tossing salads, serving customers, visiting his family and playing the part of the soon-to-be-daughter-in-law at the age of 18. I was not all in but pretended that I was. Matt was going to Winnipeg on his mission soon, and he wanted to solidify our commitment by getting engaged, and once again, Mom came to the rescue and said no. She said to wait till after he returned, and if we both still wanted, do it then. She knew better. She knew ME better.

I am grateful to have an assertive mother who was able to stand strong, even when I am sure it was really difficult to do so.

So Matt left and would write a couple of times a week. School would start again soon, and I would be less lonely. How was I going to bear this separation for two years? I was so in love, or was I?

DEPENDENCE

"How you do anything is how you do everything."

- T. Harv Eker

Little did I know I would meet my next love within days of Matt leaving Toronto at a community event a couple of blocks away from our new home. We had moved there a few months back, leaving the dingy basement for this beautiful higher floor condo space that was right on the subway line, offering so much more convenience. The spacious apartment was on a high floor with a beautiful view of downtown Toronto, and I loved it there.

It was a warm August evening. Mom and I went for a walk and heard Persian music, and we were so excited that we followed it.

There was a group of young men on stage playing Persian music, and a big crowd was dancing. At some point, I got pushed onto the dance floor by an older woman, and I found myself in the middle of a group of girls my own age.

It was love at first sight. I saw Sherry, our eyes locked, and we both smiled, and I knew that she was my soulmate. Her older sister wrote my phone number on a dollar bill using a lip pencil. I thought that was the coolest thing ever.

When I went to visit Sherry at her apartment that first time, I was awed by the ease of her life and how much fun she must be having because Sherry lived with her older sister and her older brother with no parents watching them, no adults per se. It just looked like so much fun. I fell in love with their entire family. Soon they became mine. We became attached at the hip. I wanted to spend as much time as possible with my new friends. That was the start of my young adult party life, and it was glorious. My new best friend had a big family, lots of brothers and sisters and a whole slew of fun friends. When September came, I was ecstatic when I found out that our schools were practically next to each other.

Before long, my relationship with Sherry's brother Sean took on a different feel. It was an attraction that we both felt and wanted to ignore because he was, after all, my best friend's brother. During this time, the letters from Matt continued, but he knew from the lack of response that perhaps his love for me was not mutual.

I will never forget the day when Sherry helped me write the Dear John Letter to Matt. I don't remember the content of the letter, but I remember thinking this is such a cold way of breaking up with someone I was supposed to marry. Oh well, I thought he'll get over it.

I professed my love to Sean on Sherry's 18th birthday. The same night Sean wanted to tell me that he was going to resign from this love feud because he was hurting. It was one of the most romantic experiences of my life the moment I told him that I had broken off with my ex-boyfriend and I wanted to be with him. That night we kissed and just kissed some more.

It was beautiful. I was so young and fell in love so fast and fell out of love just as fast. But it seems Sean was the one. He stole my heart forever.

DELA FOTOOHI

DAZED AND CONFUSED

*"The trick is to enjoy life. Don't wish away your days,
waiting for better ones ahead."*

- Marjorie Pay Hinckley

I actually grew up with my newfound family, all of us together. We experienced, we laughed, we cried, we lived, and we learned, all of us together. Sean was there with me all through my growing pains, always supportive, always observing, never interfering, never a roadblock. Eventually, I would take his support for granted. I misunderstood his loyalty for complacency, but that's another book.

Through those years, I watched my sweet little brother grow up into a teenager. He also had his own growing to do and his own pains to live. He also suffered and was misunderstood. I reproached him; I scorned him for his bad behaviour. The more he was reproached, the more he rebelled and the more he got in trouble. And round and round we went. I spent a lot of time worrying about him, what he was doing, who he was hanging out with. I made it my business, and it was not. I didn't understand what my job as a sister was, and so I was consumed, and I lost touch with me. I held the world responsible for my happiness, expected the people around me to cater to my emotions and slowly, I became my enemy number one. I lived in chaos with no purpose, no hope and no responsibility.

I have a few things in my life that I am not proud of. Certainly, my abortion at the age of 21, makes the top of that list. I remember the fear I felt when I found out I was pregnant. What would my mom do, what would people say, what if my life was over? I can tell you now in retrospect, that none of the reasons I had in my head, justified the fear I felt at that moment and certainly, nothing and I mean nothing was a good enough reason to terminate my pregnancy. To this day, the thought of killing my own fetus hurts me deeply and brings tears to my eyes. What I know is that I did not take responsibility for the part I had played in the predicament I had put myself in. I acted cowardly and didn't have the courage to live out the consequences of my actions then, and for the years to come.

I continued to live in fear and complacency with no passion and purpose, always pretending, always hiding behind a mask. The mask that said, "I am in control, and all is well."

The masks we wear are the masks that eventually tear us apart unless we decide to tear them up before it's too late. I wore many masks in my life. At first, because I was ashamed of my true self and too afraid to be seen as the real me. Eventually, I kept the masks because I no longer knew who the real me was anymore. So the masks got thicker and thicker until eventually, it was easier to keep them on.

And so I kept surviving. And the people around me did too. I kept busy working in oblivion, ignoring the truth and pretending I was in control. When I gave birth to my son, the fear of not being good at motherhood was overwhelming. I thought if I could just stick to the thing I know best, I won't fail. So I worked. This was my self-worth, the one thing that gave me pride since I had failed at everything else. So I overworked.

DELA FOTOOHI

MY SPIRITUAL AWAKENING

"The Soul always knows what to do to heal itself. The challenge is to silence the mind."

- Caroline Myss

When my body finally professed her objection, I finally listened. That was in March of 2016 after I had just returned from a trip, I got really sick. A few trips to the hospital and tests of all kinds showed nothing. Nevertheless, I was bedridden, couldn't keep anything down, and I was literally wasting away. I had never up to that point thought about my own mortality. How had it come to that point? I was 45 years old. For so many years, I had lived in fear, doubt, anxiety and depression. I had been dishonest, resentful, tired, frustrated, hopeless, helpless and all along had pretended that I had it all under my control. On the outside, I had it all going on, successful business, loving relationships, friends, family. Inside, though, I was empty, anxious at best, addicted to drugs and alcohol, emotionally unstable and pretentious to oblivion: a liar, cheater, selfish, judgemental and dishonest wherever I felt the need.

I look back at that trip, and I see no possible explanation of why I got so sick other than my spiritual and emotional discomforts found a way to make me realize finally how desperately ill I had gotten. This was an intervention. My body was speaking to me to cleanse my soul. And there was no other way. I had seen the subtle signs before and had ignored them wholeheartedly.

There are no coincidences; there are no accidents. Everything happens for a reason, and if we look closely enough, we always see why.

So I was sick. So sick, in fact, that it scared me because I thought I was going to die. I walked over to the bathroom and looked in the mirror and looked into my sunken eyes. They were full of life still but so fearful, so sad. I looked deep into my eyes and tried to read what they were telling me. Tears rolled down, and I was crying in agony. Not from physical pain but from some deep despair, a hopelessness that I had denied for so long. For the first time in a long time, I looked up, as we do when we are at the end of our rope, reaching for that invisible hand to pull us out of the pain. I screamed, "God, what is the meaning of this?" "What is it that I'm supposed to learn here?". Even as I said the words, I knew. The answer came so clear to me, and I had no doubt. I leaned closer to my reflection and stared into my eyes and promised, "from this moment on, I will change my life forever"!!!

I have not looked back. That was my rock bottom; it was time; it was also my big awakening, my epiphany, my breakthrough. I don't regret that trip one bit, it brought me back to life, resuscitated me, resurrected me and opened my eyes.

I don't quite know where I'd be today if I hadn't gotten sick. I don't know where I'd be if I hadn't woken up that day. All I know is that I was finally ready to live a different life, and I knew something had to change. What I didn't know was that I was about to take a whole new path, and it would have ups and downs, and it would toss and turn me every which way, and once on that path, nothing would ever be the same.

It was a weekend night in April, and I was sitting on a girlfriend's couch. Thank God for girlfriends! Thinking back to that moment, I know that it took a great amount of vulnerability for me to talk about how my life wasn't working for me and for my friend to admit that she too went through a similar experience and came to the same conclusion and shared with me her journey of rediscovering her passions and her purpose and her newfound joy. I knew right away that I wanted that. She said she had talked to a Life Coach. I had never heard of a "Life Coach" and had no idea what that was all about. All I knew was that I needed help, and I was willing to try what had worked for my friend.

One of the character traits that I am so very proud of myself for is my willingness to try new things, and my open-mindedness. And no matter what others may think of this sometimes hopeless compulsive personality trait, I think it to be the source of much joy and much more adventure.

I think that it is because of this "jumping into whatever" spirit that I was able to call Carlayne Gilbertson, and regardless of the associated cost, I knew what she had to offer was going to change my life. As a matter of fact, I have "jumped onto" more than one bandwagon. And my opinion has always been, "you never know" what is waiting for you. And this philosophy has always worked for me without severe consequences.

So here I was somewhat conservative contrary to my nature, not wanting to seem desperate, and I called the number I was given by my friend. Not knowing what this Carlayne person was going to give me and not even knowing what I wanted from her. And I knew there were some things I would never ever under any circumstances, reveal to her, no matter what!!! If you ask me today, I will tell you that I wasted the first few sessions with Carlayne. I lied, I beat around the bush, I hid my true agenda from her, and I relentlessly tried to fool her.

But I always showed up – week after week after week. Eventually, I came to trust that she was my friend, my confidant, my ally. She asked me questions that no one had asked me before, questions that sometimes were hard to answer.

At last, I spoke up. I told her my fears, my doubts, my insecurities, my flaws. I told her about my resentments, my jealousy, my expectations. I told her things I would never dream of telling anyone, and she listened, with no judgement. And the more I told her, the less I feared.

It is said that we are as sick as our secrets, and my secrets have been what made me sick. I cried every time, resenting myself, even more, wanting to stop crying, because I saw it as a sign of weakness.

I called her my angel. She was my lifeline. For so many years, I was hiding. She led me to see my power. For the first time ever, I was looking at what I needed for me. I needed a space for me, an office, a place for my thoughts and my inspirations. So I started my discovery. She coached me to dream of a place I could call my own space, with a place to sit and write my thoughts. A place that was all me, with things that meant something to me.

The day I brought my beautiful mahogany desk home was one of the proudest days of my life. I felt important that day. I felt that I had self-worth. Not because I had a desk, but because I gave myself enough value to do this for me. I swore that it was the most beautiful possession of my entire life.

I still love that desk. It has brought me so much inspiration. Thanks for the suggestion, Angel!

I started writing. I created blogs. I recorded videos — a push towards self-discovery and growth.

My beautiful mahogany desk gave me my superpower.

It is so funny how life plays out exactly how it's supposed to, like pieces of a puzzle fitting together one at a time. I was getting stronger one day at a time, not knowing that soon my strength was going to be put to the biggest test of my life.

OBLIVION

"When you complain, you make yourself a victim. Leave the situation, change the situation, or accept it. All else is madness."

- Eckhart Tolle

One of the biggest hurdles of my life then, the one thing that I blamed for the misery I was feeling was my brother. Peter was six years younger than me and had been estranged on and off from the family for the past couple of decades. Since his teenage years, he had been in and out of my life. We never got along. Our communications were few and far between, and most phone conversations were brief.

If we had contact, it was on his accord. I never understood why there were such ups and downs in his mood. Years ago, there was a diagnosis of Schizophrenia. It was always swept under the rug, though. And we never talked about it. Instead, we blamed everything under the sun for our lack of relationship.

The October after I met Carlayne, my brother, after a long absence from my life, after years of hardship, incarceration, and homelessness, had reached out for help and was staying with our mom. For years neither myself nor my mother took his diagnosis of mental illness seriously. As far as I was concerned, he was just a selfish person with a horrible attitude. It never dawned on me that he was actually ill and suffering. I was totally oblivious so much so that I often judged him, shamed him and blamed him for causing havoc in my life. I resented him for all the times he called me in a psychotic state, yelling and cursing, or to tell me that he was once again evicted or that he was taken away to the hospital or arrested and that I had to get his things or bail him out or go to court yet once again.

Only this time around when he was back into my life, I was able to get a close and frightening glimpse into his mental state and see firsthand what living with Schizophrenia did to a person. He was staying in Mom's spare bedroom, the situation was getting worse, with every passing day. He was paranoid that Mom was trying to poison him, spent the nights awake and talking back to the voices in anger and frustration banging on the walls. He would lock himself in the bathroom for hours on end as if that was the only place that kept him safe from the voices. He lashed out constantly for no reason and cursed and threatened. Mom walked on eggshells, and both of us were just plain drained and were quickly losing hope.

I knew that I needed to find help but had no idea where to start. I first approached a friend who works at a shelter in Toronto. She knew about Schizophrenia and was my first lifeline. She gave me the phone number to a place called the Canadian Mental Health Association. I remember the call I made very clearly. The voicemail said I should expect a call within two business days. I cried the entire time I was leaving the message. Within 20 minutes, I got a callback. She was compassionate and didn't take my grief for granted. She listened and suggested that I go on a waiting list for the Family Caregiver Program to educate myself on my caregiving journey. We made an appointment for an intake interview. I was basically just going on faith at this point.

I know my brother went along with me just to cooperate, but I look back at that intake appointment, and I realize I learned more in those 30 minutes than I ever knew possible. I learned that my brother was really ill. I learned that he had been hospitalized nine times during the past 12 months. I learned that he was unable to take care of himself, that he was a hoarder and had anxiety and depression, that he heard voices and had been homeless for the past two years. My heart sank right then and there, and I made a commitment at that very moment to start advocating for my ill brother.

The next couple of months were very challenging for our family. My brother stayed at mom's place; his mood was unpredictable. His rage was intimidating, and his behaviour was intolerable.

My heart was constantly racing. Every time the phone rang, I felt panic. It was hard to breathe. I couldn't concentrate. I needed help. I needed someone who understood about mental health, someone to tell me how to help my brother. I was out of options. I was tense all the time, awaiting a catastrophe. The incessant phone calls in the middle of the night and during work day were getting too much to handle. I was spent and had nothing to offer to my husband and son. Anxiety had set in. I was burnt out. Nothing seemed to be working to calm my brother. I had tried all the control strategies available to me to get him to co-operate. I had tried bullying him into seeking help. I had tried playing the victim to get him maybe to soften his demeanour. I scheduled and rescheduled appointments with the caseworker that he wouldn't keep. I tried bribing him to stay put to keep him from leaving so he wouldn't end up back on the street.

The truth was that my brother was suffering from Schizophrenia, anxiety, depression and addiction, He was in complete denial, and I was clueless as to how to help him.

FINDING ME

"When we believe our thoughts, we suffer. When we question our thoughts, we don't."

- Byron Katie

So here I was trying to find help for my brother, not knowing that I was the one who needed the help so much more. This, I would learn later, that God speaks to us through other people; that other people are the mirror in which we can see ourselves. I look back at everytime my brother said to me that I needed to change my life, that I lived a miserable life and that I was living in hell, I had always taken it so defensively or just plain ignored it and attributed it to his mean spirit and hurtful ways. Never had I stopped to think that maybe he loved me, and actually saw in me what I had missed, that he was the one who knew me and could see through my facade. The truth was that he was right but just didn't communicate it well.

And so here I was, living in total fear and in denial.

I couldn't carry on a conversation with my brother or about him with others, without crying. I thought if he would only get better, my life would be fine.

Everything happens for a reason; I believe that. In the midst of what I think to be the most trying time of my life, I found a path that would alter my livelihood in every essence.

FINDING HOPE

"God, grant me the serenity to accept the things I can not change, The courage to change the things I can, and The wisdom to know the difference."

- The Serenity Prayer

I remember driving to my very first Al-Anon meeting and passed by an alley and saw an ambulance by a fallen cyclist. It was dark, and I had no way of identifying the person, and even though I tried to convince myself of the absurdity of my belief at that moment, I was absolutely positive that the fallen cyclist was my brother. When I finally forced myself to go into that room in the church basement, my phone rang, and I dashed outside to get it because, in my mind, that was my mom phoning me to tell me my brother had been struck and was at the hospital. It wasn't, she was calling for something else, but my expectation was that there was a catastrophe waiting at every corner.

I knew I was sick, sick with my own flaws, sick with fear. I knew I was going to get help there in that room.

Right here, right now, I will tell you again, my biggest asset is and always has been my willingness to try new things, my open mind to new experiences and my belief that if I don't try, I won't know. Some might say that this sort of thinking is naive and may result in time wasted. I beg to differ, though. What if our only job in life is to live? What if we have to come into this life to experience as much as possible and to discover new possibilities? And what if we don't, because we are too conservative or we are too afraid of failing, or we have already made up our minds that nothing is going to work? I'd rather believe that the worst that can happen is Nothing.

What if we tried something new, and it worked, or it led to something else that worked?

We are here to live. That is our only purpose to live. We each have different sets of circumstances, challenges, hurdles, paths, careers, family dynamics, beliefs, purposes, passions, goals. But in the end, our only purpose is to live. Here is the choice: To do it with a smile or to do it kicking and screaming. I've come to the conclusion that it takes less effort to do this smiling than to do it kicking and screaming. I call it going with the flow.

But that's just me. You should do it your way.

When I talk about going with the flow, I am merely saying this: there are some things we can control and then there are those we can not control. The problem, the resistance arises when we think we can control everything that happens around us. Maybe this is really simple for you. But I swear up until just a few years ago, I would have laughed at this statement and challenged your thinking and declared boldly that everything was in my control. Then I walked into Al-Anon. Now some of you might not even know what Al-Anon is. In telling you this, I am actually breaking my own anonymity, but that's okay because discovering this school of thought was one of the best things that ever happened to me.

Al-Anon is based on a spiritual program. The only requirement is that you are affected by the drinking of a family or a friend. Al-Anon offers support to the families of alcoholics through a 12-step program that has been adapted from AA. Al-Anon is a free and anonymous program. At the risk of sounding too much like an infomercial, let me tell you that although they do not advertise, I truly believe that most people I meet can benefit from the teachings of Al-Anon. So if the only piece of information you take from reading my book is to find the closest Al-Anon meeting near you, then I feel like I have touched your life. AND that makes me a happy lady!

Let me start by saying that growing up in Iran during the Islamic Regime, meant that practising religion was forced. Wearing the Hijab was not a choice. Praying and fasting were not a choice. At least when in the eye of the public, We all had to pretend to be good little practising Muslim girls. The God of my understanding when I was growing up, was a God of control and vengeance. If I didn't do what he said, I would go straight to hell with all of its fires and sufferings for eternity.

Now I don't know about you, but this sort of God does not sit well with me. So when life got tough and challenges surfaced, I denounced that God. The hypocrisy is that during the most difficult moments in my life, I still relied on some force and I prayed that he/she/it would help me through this, that my brother would survive this hurdle, that my mom would get through her illness. In essence, I still turned to God when I needed some solace. When I decided to go to Al-Anon, I was grasping for some hope through a very difficult time of my life. Someone had mentioned Al-Anon for the first time, and I was going to try it as a lifeline. I remember telling my friend Kathy about it, and she warned me: Dela Al-Anon is great, just go with an open mind, because they are going to talk about God a lot. When reluctantly that October night, I pulled up to the church parking lot, I asked myself what I was doing there. This is a church Dela, I thought, of course, they are going to talk about God!!! That's okay, I am just going to try it one time, and I refuse to get baptized, I thought!!! That was three years ago. That night and then every Thursday night after that, I have thanked my stars for having led me to find out about Al-Anon.

I am merely saying here that being willing and open to life happening FOR us is so much less painful than sulking that life is happening TO us.

And so with that belief, I go with the flow.

DREAMING MY REALITY

"Never let it be said that to dream is a waste of time, for dreams are our realities in waiting. In dreams, we plant the seeds of our future."

- Unknown

I am sitting in a private jet; the sun is shining through the window. There is a table in front of me. I look down at my beige flowy pants; my high heels are luxurious and comfortable, my Burberry shawl is draping over my shoulder, I am so at peace in the moment, I know I belong there. I am alone but satisfied, at ease, confident, expectant, willing, ready. I step out onto the runway, and there is a car waiting for me. It's taking me somewhere. I sit in the car, gazing out and comfortably waiting, I know where I'm going.

Now I'm at the bottom of a few stairs that lead to the stage. I can hear the crowd in hushed anticipation, and I can feel the warmth of the stage lights. I am here to live my dream to bring them my story. I am at peace.

I have imagined myself here in this moment many times. It is as real to me as it can be. I get goosebumps as I'm writing these words.

My reality is waiting.

When I was in my twenties, I got approached by a couple who introduced me to my very first experience with network marketing. Amway was the name of the game. They made it seem so possible. We went to conferences, in big rooms filled with thousands of people waiting to hear from speakers that had made it. They knew the way. They somehow knew the secret to success and happiness. I remember feeling so enthusiastic and so energetic amidst thousands of other people. But what I really wanted, what I really dreamed of was to be there on the stage, inspiring the people, motivating thousands of spectators. I wanted to be the one that said, "If I can do this, so can you," and the crowd cheered. I wanted them to leave that room, knowing that there was nothing that was going to stop them, that there was nothing that was going to get in their way. They were going to leave that room, and they were going to make it happen. They were going to make everything they wanted come to life.

It wasn't their money or their luxury vehicles or their fancy homes and their lavish trips that attracted me. Instead, it was their charisma, their speaking power, their stage presence, their confidence that I wanted. I longed for their superpower. It was there standing in those large rooms, overwhelmed by that power that I started dreaming my big dream: one day, I'm going to be up there.

What is it about this scene that captures my heart with so much detail and so much vigour? I can see it so clearly, and I can feel it as if it has already happened. I love the feel of the fabric on my body, the warmth of the peeking sunlight, the comfort of the lush airplane seat. My heart soars with pleasure when I think about it; my eyes tear up with anticipation of the delicious image. I see it so clearly. Do you?

I have learned that we create our own reality. I have learned that the law of attraction works simply like this: we get what we think about whether we like it or not. I have read so much about the law of attraction. You can say my learning has evolved in its own way and on its own terms, always self-initiated, sometimes suggested by someone, but often one learning led to another, discovering one teacher at a time. One thing was leading to another as if by some cosmic plan waiting for me to discover their treasure chest filled with knowledge.

Teachers like Wayne Dyer, Brene Brown, Louise Hay, Marisa Peer, Esther Hicks, James MacNeil, Dr.Sayan, all walked into my life at perfect intervals and each with perfect timing as if waiting for me to be ready to receive their offerings.

And I am grateful. So grateful for all of it. That was the first lesson I learned, now not even sure to whom I should give the credit. Was it Carlayne who suggested I'd write down what I'm grateful for? Did I pick it up for the first time at Al-Anon meetings, was it Oprah? I can't remember. All I know is that starting the Gratitude Journal changed my life forever. And everything else slowly started to pour in.

EPIPHANIES

"Why do you stay in prison when the door is wide open?"

- Rumi

I remember the six-session women's group I attended as the first step towards my personal freedom. It was being facilitated by two young women, and there were five participants. Once a week, we got together and talked about a new topic, things like boundaries, self-love, self-compassion. I, for one, was totally new to all this. I took it all in like a sponge soaks up water. The topics brought up emotions that were so raw to me, things unspoken of. I cried every single time. As far as I knew, none of this was going to help my brother, who was suffering from a severe mental illness, but I knew that I was drawn to everything we were talking about. All I knew was that I wanted peace and calm, and I wanted to stop crying. I wanted a miracle to happen and something to change. I wanted to complete the course and see what would happen once I was done.

The women there were from all walks of life. There was Renee, a young French Canadian who was living with depression, among other things. She was battling addiction and abusive relationships. She showed up every single time and was right into the learning; it seemed like she already had some background knowledge about the subjects that were being brought up. Then there was Lee, an older Chinese woman who was battling her own set of problems and also was trying to end a longtime abusive relationship. She also came everytime and was a willing participant. Also, there was Yvana; she was in her forties, had a son with mental illness and was herself dealing with some social issues. We were not a healthy bunch but tried nonetheless to get better; we showed up, did the work and tried to use what we learned to the best of our ability in our lives in the hope of feeling better, finding joy and some peace of mind within ourselves.

I look back at those days and can't help but wonder, what would I have done, where would I have been, if the Bridge For Women had not started at the exact time in my life? What if I had not come across it, and had I not decided that it was worth my time and the effort it took to get there every Monday night for six weeks? I am so glad I did it.

It takes one step to start a change. I truly believe that my life changed as a result of a series of events that happened in harmony and one piece of the puzzle at a time, to get me to this moment. I know today that I have been responsible for every single event of my life. I own every single hurt I have felt. I take ownership of every mistake I made, and I know that every single experience was to get me ready for the next one. I also know today that everything happens for my own good, or did I say this already? I totally believe this with all my heart. I believe that I create my own reality. I am living proof of this, and I am creating my reality as we speak. For example, I know that this book will be published by my 48th birthday, give or take a few months.

No, I don't need a psychic to tell me this because I create my own reality. Everything I speak, I can create. Do you know that I envisioned the best Christmas ever this year? That's right. A couple of months before Christmas, as I was writing the story of the next 50 years of my life (okay, odd you say, but this was a part of my coaching journey that I absolutely loved). I wrote what Christmas day was going to look like right down to the mood of the day; I envisioned my brother and Mom sitting around the living room with me, my husband and my son relaxed, joyful, smiling, loving, exchanging gifts, sipping on Champagne. This was a dream for me; I had never imagined a day like this before, always dreaming of the day the five of us would be under the same roof relaxed, like a family. And there it was. Just like I had pictured it.

I want to convince you that you can create your own reality. What do you have to lose after all? But you have everything to gain. I have decided that if I don't like my reality, I will change it into one I want. One day, in the near future, we will all be believers; we will all finally realize how powerful human beings really are, and that we can do, and have anything we desire. One day soon, we will all know how to do exactly that.

As I started my journey of enlightenment, as I like to call my post awakened life, I was bombarded by endless messages from the universe!!! No, honestly, I am not kidding you! They came to me in the form of invitations to seminars, random YouTube videos I came across, book titles, podcasts, etc. Well, how else are you supposed to get eternal knowledge from the universe in the 21st century? So here I was, inundated with information I never had before. My discovering the Law of Attraction was one of the most significant break-throughs in my life. I lived and breathed the stuff. It made sense to me. What you most often think about, you attract.

It was then that I started taking ownership of my feelings. I learned that if I wanted to attract what I wanted, I needed to be in a good place, *i.e.*, feel good. Booooooom!

So I have made feeling good my mission. What does that mean? I catch myself when I don't feel good, and find the real reason, and then I look for the evidence of whether or not that's a valid reason. Let me tell you that most of the time, the reason I have that's making me feel bad, turns out to be totally bogus. I usually find out that the culprit was the one and only ME. This has been such a huge relief, you know why? Are you kidding? Wouldn't you be relieved too, if all of a sudden you knew that every time you felt sad, frustrated, mad, stressed, that you had the power to change that feeling just by becoming aware of it? Well, I was ecstatic!!! Suddenly, I went from being a victim of circumstances to an all-mighty, powerful being who was in charge of her feelings. I learned that if I could catch myself right then and there, and if I could find my responsibility in the reason, that I could turn that frown downside down as quickly as a whip. This meant that my route to feeling good was absolutely 100% in my own hands.

Allow me to demonstrate. One day I was driving to work. I was feeling super happy. It was a sunny day; my dog was with me. I got to the intersection, and the light turned red. All of a sudden, I heard a long and angry honk from behind. I glanced at the car beside me and saw that that car hadn't moved either, and so I knew that the light must have just turned green. In my mind, I thought, oh boy, someone is impatient, and I drove off. When I hit the next intersection, the truck behind me pulled up to the side lane to make a left turn. Now we are side by side at the red light. I could feel him looking at me. Something told me don't look, just ignore him. But I didn't listen, and I looked. He was saying something to me that didn't look loving. I rolled down the window to hear what he was saying. He was yelling, "Pay attention to the road." I couldn't resist. I said, "But it was just a second delay." to which he screamed, "It was more than a second!" Ha????

And then he drove away with screeching tires. My heart was racing; I was furious. How rude! At that moment, everything I had learned about controlling my thoughts and feelings, was dancing in a thick fog somewhere in the storage cabinets of my subconscious mind. What I wanted was not to be a rational human spirit!!! I knew better; I took a breath.

I had a choice to make; one of them involved an illegal left turn to follow him so that I could give him a piece of my mind. A better choice for me, I decided, was to keep going my way. I played the scenario in my head a few more times, and everytime I did, I shook my head with frustration at his reaction to my short delay. I realized his reaction was in my space, and I needed to clear it. I thought, "What would make a human so impatient and frustrated to react this way to a situation?" I could see so many scenarios: what if he had just lost his job? What if his child was ill? What if he had just heard bad news? Or what if he was just simply in a big hurry to get somewhere? I realized that I hadn't a clue! What made this fellow human being tick, I had no idea. I had not caused his anger; I couldn't cure his frustration, nor could I control his behaviour. All I could do was to get a handle on my own thoughts and feelings and accept what I couldn't change.

THE 3 C'S OF LIFE

From all my life lessons, the best lessons learned are the ones that I could use, all day, everyday.

This concept relinquishes control and sets you free.

C number 1 is for I did not cause it

C number 2 is for I can not change it

C number 3 is for I can not cure it

But the fourth C is for I can control me and the meaning I give to everything.

This, I learned both at Al-Anon, and the Canadian Mental Health Association and other self-development courses and workshops have taught this in some variation. One of the best lessons I have learned in my life is to let go of the desire to control others. Why is it that these sorts of things are not taught as a part of the school curriculum? I mean, who decides what our kids need to learn? I always wonder what life would be like if, alongside Geometry, we had one hour of compassion taught at school. Or along with multiplication, kids could also learn how to handle stress. Surely I am not the first genius to think of this. If you're reading this right now and you know how this can be done, please do something!

But then again, some lessons are meant to be learned along the way as "life lessons," and I appreciate that as being a part of our human experience. But think what a better experience this life would be if we taught our kids, Self-Love, Self-Compassion, Self-Esteem, Kindness, Communication, etc. All these life skills that we are expected to know, but no one takes the time to teach them. When I was a school kid back in Iran, our life skill courses were about knitting and cooking. Not that I underestimate the value of being able to sew buttons or making yogurt from scratch, but I do wish they had spent a little more time teaching me how to deal with stress. I am sure there are some schools out there who pride themselves in bringing some of these skills to their kids. But I'm talking about making this a part of the school curriculum nationwide. This way, the kids who really need it will be exposed to it also.

This may be a battle on its own, which I'm willing to explore separately from this book.

Volunteerism

Volunesia (Noun): that moment when you forget you're volunteering to help change lives, because it's changing yours.

Now let me tell you about my first act of volunteerism when I was a freshman in university. I was a volunteer in the Emergency Room at Women's College Hospital. I was 19 and wanted to apply to Med School and needed the experience.

Looking back now, I remember the pride I felt every time I was called by a nurse to run samples up to the lab or return lab results. I know that in my young mind, I was doing something important, and that gave me purpose, even though I was there for purely selfish reasons, and I quit soon after I changed my mind about going to Med School.

Volunteerism and service I've come to understand and believe are necessary for every person to grow. When we volunteer our time without asking anything in return, we are blessed. I believe with all my heart, as soon as I started giving back, my life got so much better. Whether you officially volunteer at an organization or you give your time or share your skills with others in your community, you are impacting lives in a positive way; someone is learning because you shared your knowledge, someone is feeling heard because you listened, someone is blessed because you cared.

At some point in my journey, I discovered my interest in putting myself, my words, my voice and my face out there. Although it was a vulnerable situation, I thought I was drawn to being in the public eye. So Dela's Voice started. A Talk Show that allows SuperHeros to show their superpowers.

I can tell you that as a kid, I always knew I would be famous. I practiced being loved by everyone, and in my mind's eye, I lived the life of the rich and the famous. I dreamt of my own TV Show. Only, it would be what I wanted to say and do. I was not going to act, but it was going to be real, the real me, authentic and raw. Just the way I love it. This is the stuff that the masses relate to. The real lives, the real stories of ordinary people who one day woke up and decided to live their very best and now they uplift others and show them the way to live their best lives.

In my quest to help heal the world, I have been warned that "People don't change." But I believe they do. I did. I changed. I transformed my life. I grew. I took my life into my own hands and owned my flaws and my mistakes. I did it. So can they. So can you!

Do you believe me? Do you believe me when I say there is hope at the end of the tunnel? That if you want to change, you can.

There was a time I was lost, and now I'm found.

I found myself slowly. I shed my skin and found the true me underneath. The real me that had gone dormant for so many years, asleep because it was easier. The real me hid for so many years, behind doubt, behind fear, behind fake giggles and senseless facade. The real me hid behind addiction, addiction to work, attention, validation, control, anger, jealousy, competition. Slowly the real me had disappeared, giving way to a fake image, a mirage. A poof if you will.

Then one day, I walked into Al-Anon. Can I just say, at the risk of raising some eyebrows at breaking my anonymity, I can not in good conscience keep my involvement a secret? Nor can I keep my years of volunteering at CMHA a secret. I promise to stay true to the values and not break anyone else's anonymity, though, scout's honour.

I just think of both of these amazing organizations and can't help but feel a sense of awe in the way they have the ability to impact lives and feel humbled that they impacted mine.

Because of my fear of rejection, one of the biggest risks I took was to reach out to Dr. Sayan's office and see about having her on Dela's Voice for an interview. This was a big risk for me. The thought that I was not good enough, why would she ever want to speak to little old me? She is too big for me … all freaked me out. I was afraid to reach out because I didn't want to get rejected. Dr. Sayan herself has taught me to take risks, to conquer my fears, and "to get comfortable with being uncomfortable," to create my own reality.

So I believe I will get a call from her office in California. I will make that happen. She will agree to be interviewed by me because I believe it will be of great value to her. And as for me, I just want others to learn what I learned and to become free.

This is how I learn everyday. Today, I heard that "Life is an eternal moment." Every moment is new and exciting. Today I got reminded of the necessity of childlike wonder. I got reminded that I have a creative wonder that needs to be entertained by adventure and the freedom to express itself; that if I am going to live In Joyness, I need to live without fear, without fear of hearing "no." That I need to live in a curious state, like a child, who is always wondering, without hesitation, without doubt, looking for excitement. I shall play, sing and dance for as long as this song is playing.

GRATITUDE

"Be thankful for what you have; you'll end up having more. If you concentrate on what you don't have, you will never, ever have enough."

-Oprah Winfrey

It's amazing how, at the most strange moments, I can find myself in utmost gratitude. Today, I had one of those moments. At an ultrasound appointment for multiple purposes, one being an invasive procedure, I watched as the technician explained the process as she was prepping the apparatus that looked like a dildo. She explained that even though it was clean, she was covering it with a protective coating as she pulled a condom over it. I found myself at one of my most vulnerable predicaments. I mean, in all honesty, no one likes this. To top it all, I was lying there in a paper robe and about to be probed. Yikes! I could tell she was just as uncomfortable as I, but trying to make me feel at ease by giving me the details, ever so professionally. So very vulnerable. So to escape the awkwardness of the situation, I thought a joke might come in handy. And I said, "You know, you could play a little romantic music!" As I was saying this, I was also wondering at the appropriateness of the joke. Was that okay? Was I stepping over the line? All I knew was that in that moment of pure vulnerability, I needed to be myself.

And it worked, we both started laughing, and I finally felt her relax. She said some woman had asked her if she could make it vibrate! And I thought, thank God for humour. Today, I was grateful for my humour!

If I am being honest with you, I have to say that I have changed so much. The transformation has been so subtle but consistent. Who I am today has been a gradual growth, one step at a time and some days, one step forward and two steps back. And I swear, if not for "the bigger picture," I would have given up time and time again.

Today I make Gratitude my attitude. I have understood that by being grateful, I bring more to be grateful for. It is a far cry from the way I used to live my life. Every morning I am grateful for waking up, for my health, my comfort, the love and support, the running water, the sun, the electricity, human decency, acts of kindness, smiling faces, and so much more. This has brought so much joy to my life that I often suggest that a gratitude attitude is the first step to InJoyness.

Self-Approval

"Nothing can bring you peace but yourself."

- Ralph Waldo Emmerson

One of the many habits I have kicked is looking for validation. You know you are hungry for validation when what others say or do, or you think they think of you, is all that you think and worry about. It is deeply rooted, and it starts from the time we are children. Now, I have been attending the Al-Anon program long enough to know that almost every single person who has grown up in an alcoholic home will tell you that at some phase of their lives, they looked to validation from others to feed their self-esteem and self-worth. I was so sick with this that this so-called pain inflicted by others would paralyze me for days at a time. You notice I say so-called because today, I realize that the pain was 100% self-inflicted. I remember a time when I was working at a beautiful home accessory store in a Toronto waterfront mall. The store was a wonderful place filled with beautiful things, and I loved working there. The owner was a woman in her late twenties, who was soft-spoken and fair. I was 23, with low to none self-worth, and my ego was as big as the size of the mall I worked at. This was a time when I was deeply FLAWED. I was a beautiful university student about to get married to a great guy. That summer, I had passed up the opportunity to study in Siena, Italy, because I wanted to work and save money for my dream wedding. I worked at Second Cup in the morning and at the home stores in the afternoon.

I was self-conscious in my Second Cup uniform because the pants were not cut for my shapely bum and small waist. My biggest dilemma was to walk around the mall during my breaks. I thought everyone knew me. I imagined they looked at me, judged me, and I wondered what they thought of me. Total strangers!!! Is this crazy or not? That is the power of my ego and the pain it caused me. I can now look back and say in all honesty, none of those people in the mall store or walking around the food court cared or took a second look at me. I know for sure, though, the indifference was even more painful than thinking they were judging me.

The fact that they ignored me meant that they didn't even think enough of me to notice me. So that meant that I was insignificant, not worth a second look. Believe you me, I know how ridiculous this sounds, but it's my truth, and the only reason I am revealing it is to bask in the glory of how far I have come. So don't scold my younger self, instead congratulate me, will ya? Honestly, I don't know how I survived that. I was starving. And I thought I was validated as long as I got attention. Of course, everyone uses different strategies to obtain the desired attention, and I got mine through several different ways, some of which I am not ready to reveal in my first book. And no, this is not a ruse to get you anticipating another book, but really it's because I am not yet that brave. What would you think of me??? Haha, I guess I am still a slave to people's approval!!

What I can tell you is that my need for approval got me into a whole lot of trouble with self-loathing, dishonesty, addiction, loneliness, an eating disorder, depression and anxiety.

I would love to tell you that I left all of this behind in my twenties, but I'd be lying. It has taken me years to overcome my approval-seeking personality.

No one actually teaches us these things. I mean, they might try to hint. Like when my boss said to me, "Dela, your personality is flawed." I actually said to him that he was wrong, both in his use of the English language and definitely in his assessment of my personality. I think he said something like, "You see what I mean," or something to that effect. But the people around us can hint to our flaws till they're blue in the face, but until we, ourselves, have reached the point of "Why is my life not working?" instead of "Why are people so mean to me?", nothing changes.

We always hear, "You can't change people," and we take it to mean people are always going to stay the same.

But we forget that "People change." Put the two together, and they mean, "We can't change other people unless they want to change." And that's gold. Understand this, and you have just managed to free yourself from a lifelong misery.

CONTROL

"We can not change anything unless we accept it."

- Carl Jung

Most of us want to control others. At least that's what I wanted to do, without really knowing it that is. I wanted what was best for everyone I loved after all, and since I was the smartest of the bunch, it made perfect sense to me that they should all listen to me. And guess what would happen if they didn't? Either one of two things would happen, either they would get the wrath of Dela or I would feel totally dismissed, my self worth shut down, and they would suffer the ricochet of my self wrath. Boy, oh boy, was my personality ever flawed!!

I might as well tackle the topic of "Control" right now. As a child growing up in an alcoholic home, I often felt at the mercy of circumstances. I never knew what the next hour had in stock for me, whether I would be meeting my drunk Dad or the sober one, whether it was going to be a calm household or was a fight going to erupt. I counted on my stars to keep my dad from embarrassing me. And I relied on myself to keep the peace by making myself scarce, only to find the situation turn into chaos and quickly spiralling out of my control. I slowly learned that I was powerless over the circumstances of my life. As I grew older, I tried in vain to gain control over all the situations and people that I felt I could exert power over. What I did not realize was that, if and when I got my way, it was because I threw a fit or bullied my way to getting there. And when all failed, I sulked and retreated into a corner and stopped talking.

Later, these methods continued into my adulthood, marriage and into parenthood, of course, causing an array of problems in my relationships. I really think that my people-pleasing tendencies were also my default way of keeping control in my environment, because "if you can't beat them, join them," right? So I would often say yes as a way to at least ensure my survival. And my survival so depended on whether or not other people loved me or not.

It was a vicious circle. I said yes to please others, but the more I said yes, the more I lost control of my life. The more I lost control, the more I wanted to take it back the false way, and so it continued. Until one day, I walked into Al-Anon and learned the serenity prayer.

SERENITY PRAYER

"God, grant me the serenity to accept the things I can not change, The courage to change the things I can, and the wisdom to know the difference."

How did this help me?

The serenity prayer for me is all about perspective, and perspective is everything. Disclaimer: this prayer is (as per James MacNeil) "Rated RR"- "Religiously Respectful."

To ask for the serenity to accept the things I can not control is to surrender. This was such an eye-opener for me! When I decided that there are things in my life that just are, a weight lifted off my shoulders. As a side note, this was when I also regained my spirituality and decided that by surrendering, I was relinquishing some responsibilities to my Higher Power, go with the flow and let it be.

Some things I can not control or change: the past, other people, the weather, politics, the state of economy. The faster we recognize these things, the easier the load gets. By the load, I mean hurt, anger, hatred, bitterness, despair, etc.

The second part of the prayer meant that I was admitting responsibility for the part I played in my life, my thoughts, my words and my actions, and these were the only things I could change, *i.e.*, Control. But that takes courage and is not easy, and for me, it is an everyday and ongoing task.

This new perspective was the reason for my growth, my personal development journey. Because now, I am on an adventure of discovering myself.

The last part of the serenity prayer, puts it all into perspective, mustering up the wisdom to recognize what is my responsibility and what is not. This part is a constant reminder of asking THE QUESTION: what does this have to do with me? What is my part in this? Asking myself this question in those situations when I am focusing on something outside of myself comes in very handy because right away, I can decide whether this is something that is out of my control that I need to accept or if it's something that is inward that I can change.

It is fascinating how, with a little honesty and self-reflection, we can achieve a new perspective and a new resolve.

Nowadays, I still catch myself obsessing on a subject or someone, some situation or a thought from the past or a worry for the future. I know it when I'm feeling anxious or uneasy and, overall, not right in my skin. That's when I ask myself, "What is going on with me right now?" As soon as I become aware, I am on my way to releasing my need for control.

It's quite exhilarating, actually!

One of the tools that I started using as a way to be more in control of my own thoughts and emotions was mindfulness. If you had asked me three years ago what I thought of that word, I would have told you that I had no clue. Multitasking, to me was a talent! If I could drink my coffee, talk on my cell phone all the while I was driving a stick shift vehicle, that made me feel superior in some way. Never mind that I spilled the coffee on more than one occasion and didn't really focus on the conversation on my phone and often got to my destination and wondered how I had even gotten there. Has that ever happened to you? I mean, how often do you end up in a room just to stand there and think to yourself what am I here for? That is definitely one sign that you are not being mindful. Another sign for me was that I kept banging my body parts on walls and cabinets. I would drop and break things often. I would forget appointments and names. I would forget what I was saying. I would eat, and then not even remember what I ate and how it tasted.

Today, being mindful to me means being aware of my thoughts and emotions, my bodily sensations and my surroundings, in the present moment, without judging it as good or bad, accepting it for what it is.

Not being mindful means being in my own head, drowned in thoughts, emotions, with worries from the past, anxiety for the future, not being present, not being here. When I am not mindful, I make mistakes, I am forgetful, I am stressed, I am anxious, I'm fearful, and I have no hope. When I'm mindful, I get it together. I get out of my own head. I breathe deep and come back to the moment. Becoming mindful has helped me get over some very dark moments in my life. The trick is to be aware and catch yourself as soon as you get into your head. If you don't, chances are you'll get pulled in deeper and deeper. I literally have to remind myself to shake it off.

March 17, 2020

I have to open a bracket and report on this most unusual time of my life experience. Because if I don't, years from now, People who read my book will be asking me if I was sleeping while perhaps one of the biggest events of the 21st century happened.

The Wuhan Coronavirus, or Covid-19, was the pandemic cause of 2020. Today, the schools have shut down until April 6th, companies have sent their employees home, sports events have been cancelled, university classes have stopped. People who have travelled are being asked to self-quarantine for two weeks, and travellers are cancelling their plans and staying put. We have stopped hugging, shaking hands and all touch of any kind to stop the spread of the virus. We are washing our hands more than ever and using more sanitizers than ever before. We are staying home, leaving only if we have to. Amidst all this, there are those who are taking advantage of this pandemic, to fuel their selfish needs of financial gain, or to satisfy their need for drama. They add fuel to the fire, and they thrive on public fear and panic. And then there are those who step up and take the lead on changing the conversation. They talk up the good that is still happening despite all the horrible news that is being presented. They find positivity in the middle of all that is dark. They refuse to propagate the news and instead spend their resources on spreading heartwarming words and spread calm.

These are the times we live in right now. We are having to disconnect physically from each other to avoid contamination. But we are not disconnected at all. Technology keeps us connected still. It's amazing what we are capable of. The same human mind that keeps us separate by spreading doubt and fear also brings us closer by using the most up to date technology to create virtual everything, from online workshops to online exercise classes. We are all meeting online these days. I have spent countless hours in front of my screen, talking, sharing, listening, learning, motivating, inspiring, and interviewing. I have never felt this fond of this new way of communicating. It's all great! For now!!!!

I can't help but think what if we like this new way of living so much that we might prefer it to the way things used to be. After all, if you can do the same thing you did before, but now do it from the comfort of your home, why would you get up two hours earlier, get ready, rush to get things done, only to spend one hour commuting to work in rush hour traffic and one more hour back? It doesn't make any sense unless, as humans, we need that physical connection of the warmth of a hug or the intimacy of an embrace. I might be jumping the gun here, but I feel like this is the only way for our human future – the age of

Virtual Everything. I have even thought about what the future of my business is going to look like in a few years: Virtual Floral Arrangements with the option of changing it every other day, with the appropriate scents and all. Imagine! I mean, it's pretty exciting when you think about it. While we're at it, I also want to call dibs on another novelty item: A digital screen on your window offering you your desired view from your room, giving you options between ocean-view to mountain-view, lake-view, desert or forest, depending on your likes or moods, equipped to give sounds to go with the appropriate scenes. Just imagine! If our brains can't differentiate between what is real or what is imagined, then having a fake sunny day would cure Seasonal Affective Disorder like a charm. No? I would have to do a little more research on this, but I think I might be onto something here.

Anyhow, for now, I am training to run a zoom workshop for my WW group and want to get myself into running an exercise class to replace the kickboxing classes that have been cancelled. I will report back once I do my first ones.

I wonder by the time this book is published if you are going to get to this part and laugh at the uncertainty and the deficiency of this point in time. I wonder if the new norm will just be THIS and that this would become " the way we used to do things."

Today is March 22nd, 2020.

Yesterday I ran my very set of WW virtual workshops, and even though different, the connection was still there. I showed up on camera, hair and makeup done, wearing a fascinator. The members, some of them still in bed, were in their pyjamas.

We connected, we smiled, we laughed, we sent virtual kisses and hugs. But the connection was there. We shared, we laughed, we connected even stronger. Our common denominator was what pulled us together. We found solace in the screen and offered support through the digital space. But we connected.

Tomorrow I am conducting a kickboxing class via Zoom. Here's the thing, the leaders are taking steps towards growth, the same as always, and encouraging others to come along. The leaders are the ones who are reminding others to look beyond empty supermarket shelves and toilet paper. I say toilet paper, and you might never actually know that nowadays, in the era of digital connection, people are scared senseless of running out of toilet paper. I'm not even kidding!!!

So the leaders are the ones who are reminding everyone that this is a temporary situation. A sort of a reset, you might say, Mother Earth's way of forcing a breather, a break from the high-velocity life that has had humans invested for so long, a halt to the fast-paced lifestyle we know today. The universe, God, Planet, Charma, or whatever you may call your higher power, took things into her own control and put her foot down. For the longest time, she tried to be a patient parent and watched in dismay as we misbehaved, mistreated each other, defaced the planet, abused other living things and took advantage of the resources, all the while nagging about lack, complaining about others misbehaving, sulking with ingratitude about what we thought was our right and shouting from rooftops that we somehow were justified in our attitude because, well because we just have the right to do whatever the heck we want. This is my version of what is happening and the reason it's happening.

What I believe is this: everything that happens happens for a reason. The reason is the purpose we give to everything that happens to us. Take the Coronavirus pandemic, for example. I can look at what is happening and decide that the reason this pandemic is here is to reset our humanity and the purpose it serves me will be shaped completely by me and my perspective and therefore the meaning I give it, how I live through this experience, how I deal with this part of my life, and how I will come out of this experience, will be different than the next person's experience.

The funny thing is, as the days go by, we are getting more and more used to this new way of life. A lot of people who have been working from home are finding out that they are even more productive than when they actually went into the office. Companies are realizing that instead of the overhead expenses of running their place of business, they could get more productivity by allowing people to work from home. A lot of retailers are opting to focus on their online sales. Those who never bothered strengthening their Ecommerce abilities are taking this time to explore that option. Things have changed rapidly; it seems in a blink of an eye. As if by some invisible force, we are conforming to a new norm, without questioning anything at all.

There are tons of conspiracy theorists as well, the ones who are perhaps bold enough to ask why, how, who. Some believe that COVID is a man-made virus, made by the Chinese to bring the Western superpowers down to their knees. Others believe in another conspiracy theory – connecting 5G, the fifth generation of wireless technology to the Coronavirus. Another theory is that this new virus is created as the solution to the Earth's overpopulation problem. The virus is supposed to help create an equilibrium by getting rid of the most vulnerable.

To be quite honest, I neither look for nor care to look for any support of these theories. I will, however, confess that despite my easy-going nature, lately, I question the validity of the urgency with which the media leads us to be fearful of the pandemic.

I do not wear a mask because it's not mandatory to wear one. I guess if the law says I should, I would, despite the fact that I disagree with it and also don't see much point.

In the past weeks, there has been an uproar of protests across the States because George Floyd, a black man, was killed by a white police officer, the last straw in a history of racial injustice. Vandalism, chaos and destruction have rampaged the streets. Businesses that were already suffering due to COVID shutdowns have endured even more losses due to these public uproars. People are breaking store windows and walking away with merchandise. Citizens are in conflict, using racism as the justification for their violent actions against each other.

My heart breaks at the thought of the ignorance and the hatred that humans can feel towards each other. I ask myself: what would it take for us to realize that we are all here to shine our light, and once we are gone, the only thing we leave behind is the path we have helped light up for others. And yet, I stay out of it. Silently I shake my head and ask my higher power to help me stay compassionate to them all.

My newest teacher, Meir Ezra says, every single person's actions are self-justified, because they all start with good intentions according to that individual. It's the lack of information, *i.e.*, ignorance that makes the act good or bad, helpful or destructive, benevolent or evil. Although I think it will take me a lot of years of self-growth, transcending to a higher level of consciousness, I do believe that giving this theory a possibility, eases my mind. The theory is that almost no one does anything on purpose, only to hurt another; I have also heard (I can't be sure from whom) that anything we do in life is to either bring about pleasure or to end some pain. If this is true, then there are no "Bad Guys," only "Bad Decisions." And this, although it may seem naive, is how I want to live my life. I believe this is the only salvation for humanity.

Fear comes from ignorance! Also, another Meir Ezra saying, *"We fear what we don't know."* As soon as we find out more information, we stop being fearful. I have found this to be true for me. It makes total sense, and yet we are fearful, more than just on occasion.

FEAR

"The antidote to fear is faith."

\- Dr. Wayne Dyer

Hey, did I mention that I own and operate a flower shop with my husband for the past 17 years? Starting my own flower shop was totally unfamiliar territory. When I said yes to the idea of going into the flower business with my relatives, I was 30 years old and a brand new mom. My baby boy was only three months old when I made the choice to become my own BOSS. Looking back now, I had no experience running my own business, didn't know the difference between a rose and a carnation, and certainly had never gone into business with relatives, and on top of all that, had no money to back me up.

The only thing I had a lot of was ENTHUSIASM. You heard me, my one and only amo. I was excited, had a dream, and nothing was going to stop me. One of the things that happens when I start a new project is that I get thoroughly focused on making it happen. When I have something on my mind, I just want to start, get it on the road, get the show going.

A week within making the partnership pact, I was already registered for an introductory Floral Design course, had purchased a small fridge for the flowers, had located a storefront to rent and had designed a logo. And I was on my way to becoming a florist.

If you had asked me even then, with my naive outlook on business, I knew that being a florist was not going to make me a millionaire. As it goes, being rich was never my driver in anything I have done. I think deep down, the thrill of starting something new, the adventure, has always motivated me. I have found that my tenacity in following through with ideas, creating something from nothing, and seeing it take form, shaping it into something, has always been exciting.

So as far as I was concerned, starting a flower shop was just a matter of starting one. So out came the phone book, and yes, I am that old, and I started with the first obvious item, a flower cooler.

Why you ask? Well, because that's what my gut told me. The same intuition that kept me safe all my life led me to a guy who not only sold me the most useless and the world's smallest flower cooler but also gave me the best advice a perfect stranger ever could: Sign up for an introductory course in Floral Design. The 3-week program would totally be out of my budget but the best option for me under the circumstances. So I walked into the program, with all my heart and soul and gave it all I had. What was great was that my enthusiasm was infectious, and my partners had no choice but to keep up. I learned everything

I could in those short 15 days and made it clear from the get-go that Flowers'N Things was going to open on Feb 7th, just in time for Valentine's Day.

And the rest is history.

As the years have gone by, things have changed. We moved our location, my partnership dissolved, and my husband became my work partner. We survived a couple of near bankruptcies, a road construction, numerous employee turnovers, and now we are in the middle of the current pandemic. I am still not a millionaire, but what I have accomplished is years of experience in human connection. I have learned problem-solving; I have practiced creativity in so many ways. I have built relationships and developed friendships. I have given, and I have received. I have lived in abundant beauty and comfort. I have enjoyed all the benefits of being my own boss, and I would not trade it for any paycheque. And imagine, if I had been too afraid to start in the first place!

Taking a leap of faith is necessary to follow your dreams. Trusting that if your heart is in the right place, no matter the outcome, the journey is worth it all. I don't know how long I will be operating Flowers'N Things, another year or ten more years. All I know is that the day I wake up and feel no more joy at the idea, that is the day when I know that my time is up and then, I trust that whatever happens is absolutely 100% in my own best interest.

That is faith, believing in something, even when it's hard. When you have faith, you can not fear. When you are fearful, you have lost faith. Faith in yourself, in your power, in your abilities and faith in the power that is even greater than yourself.

All through my life, even though I didn't have the words for it, I have always had faith that things will work out. Deep down inside, I must have believed that somehow, there was a force that was protecting me, and that gave me the courage to take steps forward. In my darkest moments, and believe you me, there have been a few, I always turned to that power that was bigger than myself, and prayed in my own way, asking for miracles. Sometimes what I was asking for seemed so impossible that I bargained! Yes, I bargained with my God, "God, if you help me just this once, I will never sin again." I mean, I don't exactly know the context, but I know I have done this more than once. And somehow, the problem would be solved, and I would be saved. There was a time in my life when I started smoking pot. What started as an occasional fun thing, slowly became my go-to solution when times got tough. Before I knew it, a whole decade had gone by, and I was a solid pothead. I mean, of course, I wasn't admitting that I was. Honestly, I even lied to myself. I don't know if you have ever had that experience, but you know you have an addiction when you are constantly trying to quit. That was me! Every time I smoked, I swore that was my last one, and the next day I was back at craving that hit. I would have all these intentions, goals, things I wanted to accomplish, and they seemed so important to me when sober. A few puffs later, none of them mattered. And days, weeks, months, years went by. I smoked to get energized, to relax, to get in the mood, to wind down, to be more creative, to have fun. But really, I smoked to hide away from myself.

What I learned from my dazed and blurry days, is that no matter what variety of distraction we lean on, whether a substance, work, TV, etc., it is a temporary relief from what is truly going on inside.

It's fear that pushes us to rely on a distraction, the fear of facing whatever it is we have to face. For me, I was afraid to face my truth. Everything was so much better after I smoked. Life was beautiful again; my troubles didn't seem as bad. And most of all, I didn't care. At least until the next sober moment.

I was in denial that my life wasn't working. After all, I had pretended for so many years that my life was perfect and that I was living a fairy tale that even I believed.

The day I stopped was bittersweet. I had finally made the decision and was so proud of myself, and I was scared out of my wits about how I was going to face my life. I realized that the day I relied on the fix, was the day I had quit on my faith, it was the day I gave in to fear.

And now, I had to have faith again that things were going to get better.

Do you remember what I had said before about the statement," I didn't know"?

Well, it turned out I used this for an excuse for every time I made a mistake because of an oversight or inexperience, but also every time I ignored my better judgement and did what I did, even though the consequences were clear to me. The moment I learned to take responsibility for my actions, the words "I didn't know," stopped to exist in my vocabulary. Today I know that when faced with decisions to make, that I always know. I know deep down inside whether something I am about to say will hurt someone, I know whether what I'm about to do is right or wrong. We always know, because intrinsically we are wired to do the right thing.

In the words of Meir Ezra, *"YOU are perfect, and everything that is not perfect is not you."* And so, whenever I think, do or say something that is not in alignment with who I am, I know.

Realizing that we are perfect, has been one of the most important stepping stones in my life. This allows me to see others in their perfection and know that when they do or say something imperfect, it is not them. I can appreciate that everyone starts off with good intentions for themselves, and if they end up "committing a sin," it is because they had the wrong idea. I realize that what this means is that there are no "bad" people in the world, and this sort of thinking will exonerate even the worst criminals. And this might be too much to swallow for a lot of people. In any case, I resonate with this philosophy, and I am simply relaying it here. I choose this because I would rather think that human beings are intrinsically good rather than evil.

DELA FOTOOHI

MY TRIPLE-A SUCCESS FORMULA

"To love oneself is the beginning of a lifelong romance."

\- Oscar Wilde

My name is Dela Fotoohi, and I am the Host of Dela's Voice Talk Show.

I am one of those blessed individuals who is living her passion in life, doing what I love and loving what I do. I am also impacting the world in a positive way by bringing information, inspiration and motivation for wellness and recovery through what I do as a talk show host. I am truly blessed.

But Not too long ago, I didn't feel this way, even though I have always been blessed with so much grace in my life. I just didn't see it this way.

The story I told myself was that I was a victim of circumstances, that I didn't have enough love and support, that my life was meaningless. I blamed everything and everyone for all that was going wrong in my life. There was a time that I suffered deeply with self-loathing, self-blame, shame, depression and anxiety.

I want to say that I don't regret living the life I did, because had I not lived that, I wouldn't be here today writing about it. I truly believe that we live better when we know better. I am also feeling blessed because I am still here, able to write about my experience. And in doing so, I hope it might spark a soul or two and at the risk of being bold, millions.

If I have learned anything at all from all the people I have interviewed, it is the fact that every single person has a story to tell. Everyone I have talked to on Dela's Voice has had struggles. They all have lived through trials and tribulations. They all faced challenges, some more than others, but a challenge nonetheless. They had a moment in life where they experienced an awakening, made a shift, and they took a step.

And although the stories are different, the life lessons are the same. What I hear over and over again are lessons in courage, resilience and persistence, vulnerability, love and brilliance.

All of these individuals have discovered that they are only joyful when they're living their passions, and for 100% of them, creating an impact is also a part of their passion.

When I talk to them, I am awed by their tales; I gasp at their hardship, I hold back tears of compassion for the hurt they felt and cries of joy at their victories. I ignite with their account of breakthroughs and get inspired when they tell me how they got to their current destination.

I am so blessed by my predicament.

But the best part for me is that I learn every single time. I have learned about Nutrition, Health, The Law of Attraction, Homeopathy, Energy Healing, the art of Fung Shui, Quan Chi, NLP, Hypnotherapy, Quantum Physics, Integrative Medicine, Meditation, Yoga, Motivational Speaking, Writing, Financial Coaching, Transformational Coaching, Success Coaching, Performance Coaching, Tapping, Real Estate and so much more.

I have learned from the very best in the field. And I look forward to every single encounter and more deep learning.

These people have mastered their art and are using it every day to change lives.

One thing is certain: Time and time again, I have tested my theory and have proven to myself that in order for these Masters to help, the clients have to be ready and not a second sooner.

This is how I came up with my Triple-A Success Formula (Trademark). Of course, the first time I was introduced to the three A's was at the Al-Anon program. They used the formula to pinpoint personal responsibility in recovery. My own version of the three A's is slightly changed because I wanted something that would speak to every single situation, whether it was to achieve recovery from addiction or any other situation where a person feels stuck.

So here we go. This is a complete definition of my Triple-A Success Formula. Use it as you see fit in your life.

The first A is for Admit. I believe that the first step to start any change is to admit that there is a problem. Whether that problem is in your relationship at home, at work, in your social life, or whether the problem is that you have an addiction, or that you are overweight, or that you are just not happy for any reason at all.

It's amazing how many of us live complacent lives because we just don't believe that there is a choice. We go to work, we come home, we watch TV, we eat, we go to sleep ... and we look forward to our retirement so that one day we may live. The sad part is that that's just an illusion. And if nothing changes in us, how is Retirement going to bring us any joy? So we live in Oblivion, and we are miserable.

As I keep hearing over and over again that "The Nile"[pronounced Denial] is a river in Egypt, and Denial is not. So many of us spend most of our life in a state of psychological denial, and for as long as we are there, absolutely nothing will ever change because we are closed off to all other possibilities. So the first step is to Admit there is an issue. For me, when I admitted to myself that my life was a disaster, and I was in a state of despair and hopelessness, I was ready to accept change but not one second before.

As for me, I lived in agony for years. I had no clue that I could live a better life. I just knew that I was not happy, and I blamed the world for my unhappiness. I knew that I wanted things to be better, but I couldn't admit that, because that would have meant that I had failed at life. The day I admitted that I was no longer okay with living like this was the beginning of my life. I truly believe that that's the moment I started living. A is for admitting that there's a problem, that there is something that is not working, that there's an issue that needs addressing. And that's the moment of truth. In reading this part, my ultimate hope is that you find the courage to admit and acknowledge if you are not living your best life.

The second A is for Ask.

Trust me when I say that I understand the pain you have to endure as you open up to sometimes, complete strangers and talk about being vulnerable. We have all these preconceived notions about what would happen if people found out that we may be judged or shunned and rejected. What if we lose our friends, and no one would ever want to talk to us? Right? I know, that was me. Vulnerable yes, shunned no! At least that was my experience.

Now I have to tell you that asking for help is out of most people's comfort zone, especially if they are used to pretending that they're always in control of their lives.

Asking for help takes courage. Asking for help means you have to be vulnerable. Asking for help is saying, "This thing that I am dealing with is bigger than me, and I can't manage it on my own," and that's difficult for most people.

When I asked for help, three things happened for me:

Number one: I found out that I was not alone. Most people I talked to were very familiar with what I was going through. As I opened up with honesty and courage, so did they. I have developed many strong relationships because of the bond that was created once I could be vulnerable. I created a support system with people who I trusted.

Number two: when I opened up and asked for help, I learned there were many resources available to get help. For the most part, this gave me hope. HOPE: The four-letter word that literally for me meant: HOLD ON, PAIN ENDS. This was a time in my life when I needed to have hope, and asking for help brought me hope.

Number three: asking for help also helped me strengthen myself. I developed my own voice. I discovered that being heard was powerful and so essential in my recovery journey. So I started opening up more and talked about my struggles and soon found out that I was also the voice for others. The more I spoke up, the stronger I got. As I found my voice and learned how to get my message out there, I was able to impact the lives of others.

The third A is for Action and the most difficult part of the formula. It takes a lot of motivation, commitment, persistence to take action everyday to change your life. Every single step you take towards change hurts. Change is like shedding layers, and it's uncomfortable. You have to step out of your bubble, your familiar space, in order to change. We change at our own pace based on the action we take. What might take one person to achieve in a lifetime may be achieved by another in a year. As much as we like to get to our goals as quickly as possible, it's important to remember that life is not a competition and that the only person you need to compare yourself to is the person you were yesterday. Keep that in mind, and you might actually enjoy the process and your progress in this journey.

When I took action toward my recovery, I started hearing words like self-compassion, self-love, self-limiting beliefs. I heard terms like boundaries and detachment. I heard about self-blame and self-forgiveness. These unfamiliar words were so outside of my comfort zone that in order for me to implement them in my life, I needed reinforcements. I did that in the form of workshops, webinars, seminars, courses, programs, coaching and more coaching, podcasts, books; you name it I did it. It has taken me years and thousands of dollars invested in me to grow into the person I am today. I have never regretted the life I have lived because if it weren't for all of my journey, I would not be typing these words on these pages. What I am here to tell you is that taking personal responsibility towards your own growth is the best gift you can give yourself and the people you love, because when you change, the people around you also change. That's a guarantee. I have never been more fulfilled and joyous. I have never had better relationships, and I have never been more passionate about life than at this very moment. If this is not success, then I don't know what is.

What I hope is that reading this chapter will ignite something in you that will result in changing your life toward the best life you can live. That is my ultimate hope.

If you found it helpful, please feel free to use my Triple-A Success Formula in your life as much as possible and share it with your friends and loved ones. May it reach millions of people across the globe.

As a matter of fact, here is a little gift! Go ahead and download the free PDF to my Triple-A Success Formula. You will also have access to a guide that will help you start your own recovery journey. Following is the link: https://bit.ly/2Dqe9o8

Here's to your success in living InJoyness.

This is Dela's voice Hoping to Spark Your Soul. Till next time.

In Gratitude & Love

-Dela

INJOYNESS